Galax Dulcimer

A Job of Journey Work

Phyllis Gaskins

Layout and Editing - Brent M. Holl
Editing Assistance - Karen F. Holl and Jim Gaskins

Printed and Distributed by
Fingers Of Steel
FingersOfSteel.com

ISBN 978-1-964725-56-7
© 2012 Phyllis Gaskins. All rights reserved.

No part of this publication may be reproduced, stored in a retrieval system or transmitted in any form or by any means, electronic, mechanical, photocopying, recording or otherwise, without the prior permission of the copyright owner.

This book of tunes has been a labor of love for an instrument, its music, and its maker.

During the 1970s and into the early 1990s, my husband Jim and I spent our summers traveling from one fiddler's convention to another in Southwestern Virginia, Western North Carolina, Tennessee, and West Virginia. Through these travels, we established friendships with such fiddlers and banjo players as Luther Davis, Abe Horton, Tommy Jarrel, and Albert Hash, to name but a few. At these conventions I met my mentor, Raymond Melton.

With a turkey quill flashing across the strings of a large mountain dulcimer, Raymond played the melody line of the fiddle tunes right along with the fiddle and banjo in a string band, The Blue Sky Ramblers. He used a flat hard wooden stick as a noter and a shaved turkey quill for strumming. Fascinated, I watched him play and noticed he rarely looked down at his hands while always smiling out at the crowd surrounding the band! I spent many hours at his side learning his technique and absorbing his tunes. How I miss those hours of jamming with him.

During that time, Jim and I also spent a Saturday each month at the Galax (pronounced "gay - lax"), Virginia, home of the fiddler, Luther Davis, 92 when we met him. We learned some of his more obscure versions of tunes, which we love to play.

Remembering the musicians from whom I learned particular tunes is important. I have included information about when and where I learned some of these special tunes. You will also see some photos of those special friends who contributed to my musical journey and repertoire of tunes. Some of these tunes trace back hundreds of years, others have no written history, but all these old tunes are a part of history passed from one generation to another, thereby continuing the life of the tunes.

Having entered the world of Virginia's traditional music and having enjoyed exploring the ancestry of many tunes, Jim and I strive to maintain authenticity in our playing of the tunes. Here I pass the tunes and style of playing on to you, and thus, our lives entwine in the sheer joy and exhilaration of learning and playing.

Phyllis W. Gaskins

(Photo: Steve Zapton)

1	My First Melton Dulcimer
3	My "Aha!" Moment Connecting The Hummel And The Old Galax Dulcimers
6	The Galax Fiddler's Convention, The Melton Family, And Virginia Dulcimers
9	Galax Dulcimer Body Design And Construction
13	Playing The Galax Dulcimer

15   Playing D Tunes On The Galax Dulcimer

16	Big Liza Jane		24	Katy Cline
17	Black-Eyed Suzie		25	Luther's Walking In The Parlor
18	Chapel Hill March		26	Old Molly Hare
19	Ducks On The Millpond		27	Old Time Sally Ann
20	Fortune		28	Peek-A-Boo Waltz
21	Green Willis		29	Sugar Hill
23	Julie Ann Johnson		30	Walkin' In The Parlor

31   Playing G Tunes On The Galax Dulcimer

32	Dance All Night With A Bottle In Your Hand		38	Long Journey Home
			39	Merriweather
33	Did You Ever See The Devil, Uncle Joe?		40	Sandy River Belle
34	Ebenezer		41	Seneca Square Dance
35	Evening Star Waltz		42	Silly Bill
36	The Girl I Left Behind Me		43	Unclouded Day
37	John Brown's March			

44   Playing A / A-Modal Tunes On The Galax Dulcimer

45	Breakin' Up Christmas		52	New Castle (Texas)
46	Cluck Old Hen		53	Sail Away Ladies
47	Cold Frosty MOrnring		54	Sally Goodin
48	Dinah		55	Sheep Shell Corn
49	Falls Of Richmond		56	Sugar In The Gourd
50	Highlander's Farewell		57	Train On The Island
51	Kitchen Girl			

58   Playing Two-Key Tunes On The Galax Dulcimer

59	Flop-Eared Mule		60	Jenny Lind Polka

61	Roscoe Russell Galax Dulcimer And Keith Young Early Virginia Model
62	Ben Seymour As Galax Builder
62	An Interview With Don Neuhauser
64	Terry Burcham's Jacob Melton Dulcimer
65	Raymond V. Melton Patterned Galax Dulcimers By Bowlen And Gaskins
66	Recordings By Phyllis Gaskins
67	Dedications And Acknowledgements
68	About The Author

My First Melton Dulcimer

My journey with the Galax Dulcimer started when I saw Raymond Melton playing his dulcimer at various fiddler's conventions. I already owned a Bob Mize mountain dulcimer with a heavenly sound which I had purchased in 1974. Jim and I went to our first fiddler's conventions and dulcimer events in 1975 where I watched and played with other mountain (lap) dulcimer players.

All of the lap dulcimers, including the Galax Dulcimer, which is only one type of Virginia dulcimer, as well as the Tennessee, Kentucky, North Carolina, and West Virginia dulcimers are mountain dulcimers. Each maker from each of those states had his own family style/shape and we can tell the old dulcimers from these makers by their unique characteristics. The distinguishing characteristics of the various dulcimers are discussed in other books (see p. 8 if you want further sources about those dulcimers). I intend in this book to tell you about one dulcimer style from the Galax area of Southwest Virginia not discussed in much detail in any other book.

I had heard and played on those smaller dulcimers, but watching and listening to Raymond play lightning fast fiddle tunes on his big dulcimer for the first time was an epiphany. When I met Raymond Melton, no one called his instrument a Galax Dulcimer. Raymond called it a Melton-style dulcimer as it was patterned after dulcimers his family had been making since at least the mid-1800s. Roscoe Russell, another prominent Galax Dulcimer builder, learned to make these dulcimers from Raymond Melton's family and was also making them in the 1970s-1980s. The Melton dulcimers could be distinguished from the Russell dulcimers by the body and head shapes.

Phyllis playing the dulcimer she made with Audrey Hash in 1978.

I asked Raymond to make me a dulcimer in 1977, and each time I saw him at a fiddler's convention, he would assure me he was going to make one for me. He made dulcimers regularly and usually had a couple in the trunk of his car for sale. On several occasions during the many treks to local fiddler's conventions, I thought I was really close to getting one of his dulcimers. He would open the trunk of his car, and I would ask if I could buy one. He always said, "No. I'll make you one sometime."

During this time when he saw me walk up to jam sessions he had with the Blue Sky Ramblers and others, he would say to me, "Come here, girl. Sit down! You don't know how to play that thing!" At the time I was using an hourglass-shaped dulcimer, and I was trying so hard: watching, listening, and taping those tunes. He never slowed anything down for me. He just kept playing and smiling. I guess that was part of the fun and challenge for him and me.

I wanted one of the big Galax Dulcimers so badly that in the summer of 1978 I asked Audrey Hash-Miller, the daughter of the fiddle maker, Albert Hash, to help me make one. I drew what I thought would be a "close enough" body shape. We used her head and tailpiece patterns, put on four equidistant .010 gauge strings, and away I went! The next time I saw Raymond I showed him the dulcimer and told him what I had done. Again he told me he would make me a dulcimer, but he would not sell me one from the trunk of his car.

Finally, the big day came. Raymond said, "I made that dulcimer for you."

"Great!" I shouted. "Where is it?"

"It's at the house," he replied in his calm, gentlemanly manner.

"Okay," I said. "Where do you live?"

To which he replied, even more calmly and firmly, "You'll find it."

Strangely, after years of playing together every weekend through the festival seasons, Jim and I had not visited Raymond at home. He was a very reserved and private person who did not like to have musician friends over to the house. We made several inquiries in Woodlawn, and we did "find it." We just dropped by his house. When his wife, Oma, let us into the house, as if expecting us, Raymond fetched the dulcimer, made of beautiful, rare chestnut wood he had salvaged from an old barn. I asked him to play it for me, and he did.

He said confidently, "It's the best one I ever made, and you're gonna beat me on it someday." That was in 1980. In 1982, everywhere we competed, I took first place, and he took second. As first and second place winners at the Galax Old Fiddler's Convention that summer, we were invited to go to the 1982 World's Fair in Knoxville, Tennessee, to compete in a mini-fiddler's convention.

Dulcimer given to Raymond and his wife as a wedding gift from his uncle.

On the day I picked the dulcimer up at his house, Raymond shared with me other dulcimers his family had made. A black one had been given to him as a wedding gift. He told me some of the Melton family dulcimers had been diamond shaped and others were shaped like his pattern.

Raymond told me he needed the 6.5 fret for playing in string bands and jam sessions, so he put it in. His dulcimers were the first that I had ever seen with a 6.5 fret. It sure makes going from the key of D to the key of G easy.

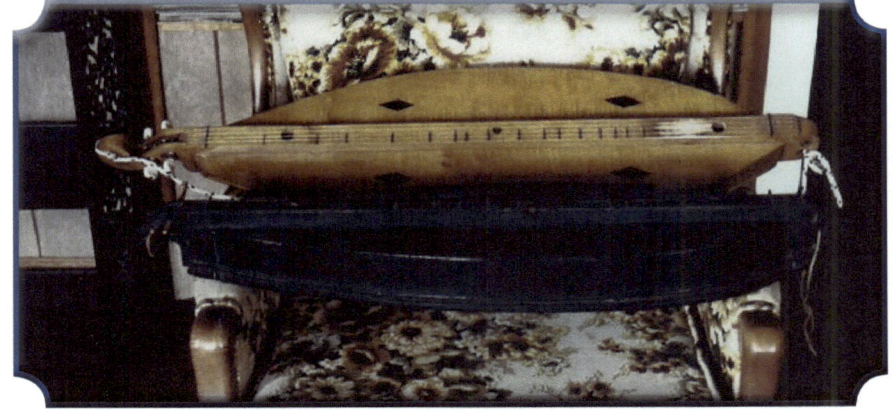

Raymond shared these two dulcimers with me when I picked up my new instrument. The maple dulcimer is his personal instrument with which he won many contests. You can see the strumming marks made by the turkey quill. The black dulcimer was his mother's instrument.

My "AHA!" Moment Connecting the Hummel and the Old Galax Dulcimers

Learning the old-time Melton style of dulcimer playing in the 1970s, I was the "odd man out" with my Galax "boat." I watched others learning and teaching mountain dulcimer techniques using single bottom, hourglass-shaped or teardrop-shaped dulcimers from the Tennessee, Kentucky, or North Carolina traditions with a three-string pattern: light, medium, and heavy gauge strings. Those smaller-bodied dulcimers produced softer tones and were difficult to hear when played in jam sessions with other instruments. The Melton family style seemed so unrelated to those instruments and styles of playing that a fellow dulcimer player said to me, "Why don't you get yourself a REAL dulcimer?" In anger and defense I retorted, "This IS a REAL dulcimer! YOU just don't know it yet!"

Those were fairly prophetic words coming from someone who then knew little about the history of dulcimers. You see, the Melton family had been making and playing this style of dulcimer during the early to mid 1800s. Yep! This dulcimer is one of the oldest (body shape, tuning set up, and strumming technique) for which we have primary source data. Why, one wonders, were these dulcimers so different from the others? (Remember, these are Melton family style, or Old Virgina dulcimers; the name Galax Dulcimer came later.)

Let's go back to the 1700s and the movement of German settlers into then "Old Virginia" (now West Virginia and Virginia). Our German ancestors brought into the Great Valley of Virginia and across the valley and ridge region of what is now West Virginia an instrument known as a fretted zither, or scheitholt. These instruments had no raised fret board and included varying numbers of additional strings for droning/chording. They are well referenced in **Appalachian Traditions** (Ralph Lee Smith), **A Catalogue of Pre-Revival Appalachian Dulcimers** (L. Allen Smith), **The Story of the Dulcimer** (Ralph Lee Smith), and **Play of a Fiddle** (Gerald Milnes). I enter the discussion about these mountain dulcimer "ancestors" with only this statement: I, along with numerous historians and researchers, believe these were the ancestors of our mountain dulcimer and the Galax Dulcimer is one of the earliest of these dulcimers.

In 2009 I had an AHA moment when the German ancient instrument restoration luthier, Wilfried Ulrich, shared with me pictures of an interesting German instrument, a hummel, he had restored for a German museum. He also showed me a beautiful instrument he had built, a replica of one of the old museum hummels. On his replica (like the authentic one pictured below), the first four strings were all the same light gauge! Now I knew why the old Melton dulcimers had a mono-tonal tuning with four strings of the same gauge.

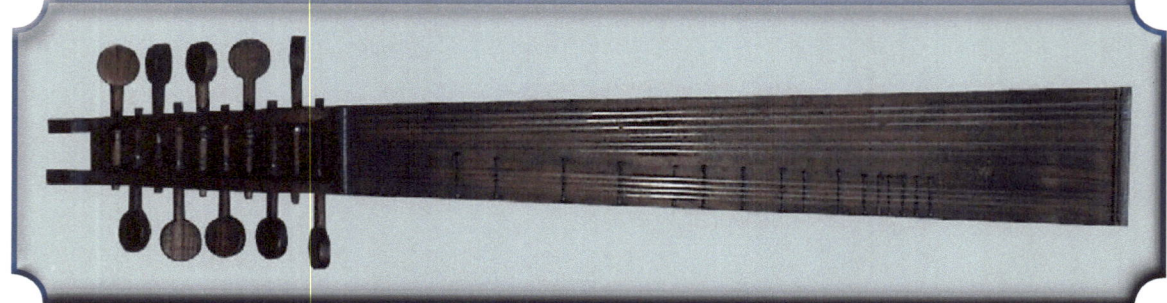

On this 1871 Adolf Hilke hummel, restored in 2004 by Wilfried Ulrich and now in the Museum Northeim, note the four equidistant strings of the same gauge. (Photo: Wilfried Ulrich)

The Meltons had used the first four strings from an old German instrument for their style of building and playing the instrument. These Old Virginia dulcimers were set up with staple frets only under the two melody strings with the other two strings of the same gauge acting as drones just as many ancient fretted zithers were set up. On the fretted sections of the old German zithers/hummels/scheitholts, four (sometimes five) strings of the same gauge were melody strings noted with a wooden noter with additional strings becoming heavier in succession. Makers of the Old Virginia dulcimers, and makers of the Galax Dulcimers in particular, used this ancient equidistant set up for the four strings of their instruments, putting staple frets only under the two melody strings. The other two strings of the same gauge provided a drone accompaniment. All of the other heavier gauge zither strings were eliminated. Other mountain dulcimer makers seem to have used a mix of the first one or two strings with the heavier outer strings.

Wilfried showed me a photo of a facsimile of an old advertisement for a German hummel. The player used a flat noter to note the first two strings of the instrument; the index finger was placed on top of the noter immediately above the two noted strings. AHA! That is exactly the traditional way of noting the old Galax Dulcimer. The tuning and noting in that moment connected in my mind to that ancient German ancestral instrument.

This reproduction shows Adolf Hilke noting across all four equidistant strings for the melody. Note the index finger on top of the wooden noter just as the majority of older traditional Virginia players held their noters. (Photo: Wilfried Ulrich)

Wilfried restored this 1758 Friesische Hummel in 2010 (displayed now in Museum Flensburg). Here again the first four strings are equidistant and of the same gauge for noting the melody. More of these interesting, restored instruments can be seen in Wilfried's book, (website http://www.ulrich-instrumente.de/). (Photo: Wilfried Ulrich)

The well-known dulcimer maker Keith Young made a replica of an Old Virginia instrument that dates back to the mid-1700s. This dulcimer has the same mono-tonal, equidistant string set up with staple frets only under the first two strings as did other old, historically documented Virginia dulcimers, including those from makers of the extended Melton family.

Keith Young recreated this early Virginia style Appalachian dulcimer as they were built in the mid-1700s. It has handmade cleat frets under the first two strings for playing the melody (26" vibrating string length). (http://appalachiandulcimers.com/appdul.htm)

On the fretboard of my cherry dulcimer made by Raymond Melton, you can see the four equidistant strings and the "ladies' hairpin" frets under the first two melody strings. Raymond shaped "old timey steel hair pins" into frets for his dulcimers.

The Galax Fiddler's Convention, the Melton Family, and Virginia Dulcimers

"Galax Style" denotes both a type of mountain dulcimer and a style of playing made famous by the Meltons and their relatives from Galax in southwestern Virginia. In the first forty years of the Galax Old Fiddler's Convention, the Meltons used their dulcimers to play fast and furious tunes just as fiddle players did in the string band tradition, thus winning most of the top prizes in the dulcimer competitions there. Because of the many dulcimer competition winners playing this style and type of instrument during the 1970s, this dulcimer is known as the Galax Dulcimer.

The Galax Dulcimer, one of the oldest in the history of mountain dulcimers, was virtually bypassed during the dulcimer revival of the 1960s. Jean Ritchie, the most important, influential figure in the revival and growing popularity of the mountain dulcimer, performed on the world stage, causing an exploding interest in the dulcimer. Many innovative young players took to the instrument and quickly developed contemporary styles of playing that moved far beyond the traditional ballads and songs introduced by Jean Ritchie. In 2001, when she and I were both on the dulcimer staff at the Swannanoa Gathering Dulcimer Week, I talked briefly with her about meeting Raymond Melton. She told me they had met at the Folklife Festival in Washington, D.C., many years before when they each represented a family music heritage. She was glad to hear I was carrying on the tradition. I was honored and grateful for that moment.

Raymond Melton, the family "torch bearer" of this old Virginia style of playing in old time and bluegrass music bands, played the tunes and songs of the secluded mountainous region of southwest Virginia where he was born and raised. Once Raymond told me, "I play the old tunes, and I play the tunes I like." He could play an old hoedown or a popular country song from the radio, all good music to him. There was always joyfulness in his playing of the tunes.

Many members of Raymond's family also played in the Galax Old Fiddler's Convention dulcimer competitions over the years. The winners of the first dulcimer competitions all connect somehow to the Melton family. (Winners' list taken from **The First Forty Years of the Old Fiddler's Convention**.)

1935 - 1st: Ruth Melton, 2nd: Tina Melton
1936 - 1st: Jacob Melton (Raymond Melton's older brother), 2nd: Lina Melton (Jacob Melton's wife)
1937 - 1st: Raymond Melton, 2nd: Belva Nester
1938 - records lost
1939 - 1st: Raymond Melton, 2nd: Velma Musser, 3rd: Jacob Melton
1940 - 1st: Raymond Melton, 2nd: Tina Melton
1941 - 1st: Blanch Melton (Pierce Melton's daughter), 2nd: Ray Melton (Jacob's son), 3rd: Jacob Melton
1942 - 1st: Blanch Melton
1943 - 1944 World War II and no Galax Fiddler's Convention

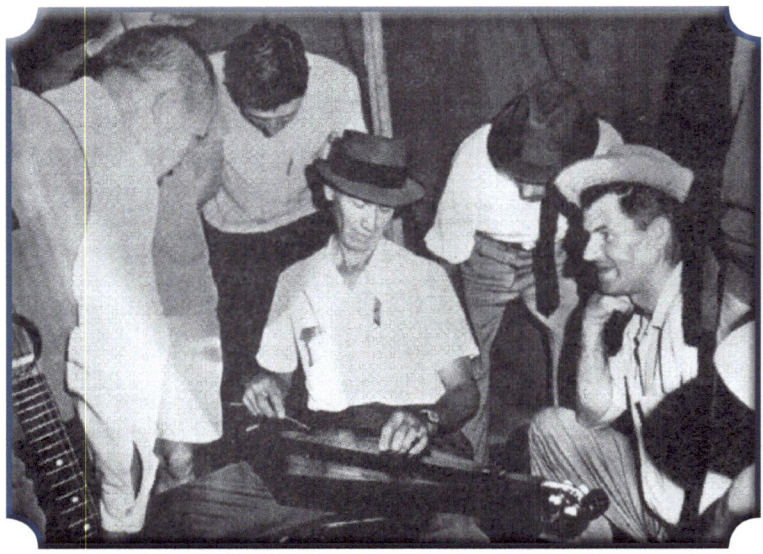

From **The First Forty Years of the Old Fiddler's Convention** (Herman K. Williams, Galax, VA), this photo shows Raymond Melton, probably during the 1940s, playing one of the old diamond-shaped dulcimers for pleased on-lookers. Notice the banjo tuners on the peghead.

When the Fiddler's Convention resumed after WW II, the dulcimer competition was not an individual category; however, Raymond told me he attended all those years and played at every convention. In 1974 the dulcimer competition resumed, and the winners again are related to the Meltons.

1974 - 1st: Bonnie Russell (daughter of Roscoe Russell and his wife Ruth Melton Russell)
      2nd: Raymond Melton
      3rd: Terry Burcham (playing a dulcimer made by Jacob Melton)
      4th: Roscoe Russell
      5th: Velma Musser

Coincidentally, I first purchased a dulcimer in 1974. A year later I saw Raymond, and then my dulcimer adventure really started!

In 1980 I purchased my first Galax Dulcimer from Raymond. In 1982 I took first place at Galax and Raymond took second. By then, a deep friendship and strong musical bond had developed between us.

In 1985 as we were standing in line under the contestants' tent, I was laughing and talking with Raymond. "I guess we'll be standing here again next year," I said.

"Nope," he replied. "I've been to every one, and this is my last." He died two months later.

Around 1990, I stumbled upon "Harmon's Museum" in the back room of a store called Harmon's Western Wear in Woodlawn, Virginia, an amazing place with photos, furniture, and other relics from days gone by. There to my left on a table not too far from the fireplace (very ironic since dulcimers are descended from the scheitholt which means "fire wood!" I just had to smile.) were some instruments made by Raymond and members of his family. My fellow musician friend, Charlie Shaeff, just happened to shoot the following black and white photos the day we went to Harmon's. Thanks for sending me the photos, Charlie!

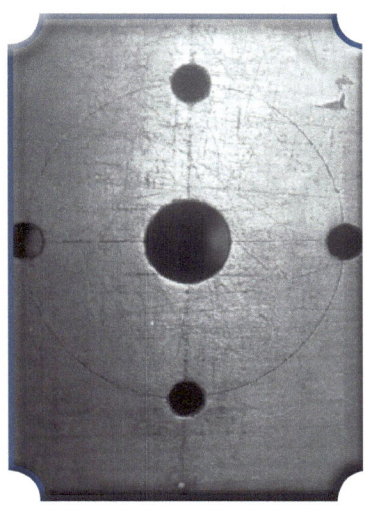

This back section of one of the old Melton dulcimers has extra sound holes put there to "let the sound out."

Yet another relative of the mountain dulcimer, this instrument, appropriately enough, sits near the fireplace. Awaiting its destiny?

The label for this instrument says: Made by Raymond V. Melton. The dulcimer has the same diamond shape as his wedding gift. I noticed Raymond had stopped putting on the double bottom, a feature of his family's early dulcimers. When I asked him why, he told me, "My dulcimers are loud enough without it."

Notice the pegs are not wooden. The very practical Meltons replaced wooden pegs with mechanical tuners very early, sometimes using mandolin tuners cut to fit or old style guitar tuners. Even banjo tuners can be seen on some of their instruments.

Galax Dulcimer Body Design and Construction

The Galax Dulcimer is, as Ralph Lee Smith describes it, an enlarged version of a single bout Virginia dulcimer, often with a "double" bottom. The Galax Dulcimer has a specific body shape, construction features characteristic of the older Melton family dulcimers, and a special string set-up.

Specific features
- » four equidistant strings
- » all strings of the same gauge (0.10)
- » a double bottom
- » a hollow one-piece head/fretboard/tailpiece design
- » a D-shaped tailpiece
- » staple frets only under the first two fretted strings
- » a 6+ (6.5) fret on Raymond Melton's dulcimers

Four Equidistant Strings of the Same Gauge
Virtually all of the traditional Virginia dulcimers I have seen made by the Meltons and the Russells have been strung up with 0.10 gauge strings, which produce a very bright bell-like tone, great for fiddle tunes played in D and G. Raymond did make an exception on his A dulcimer. He used a lighter gauge string tuned to E for playing his A tunes with "do" on the 3rd fret.

Double Bottom
For acoustic purposes, almost all of the old Melton and Russell dulcimers had double bottoms; many had laminated wood bottoms which hid the beautiful natural wood sandwiched between the second bottom and the top. Roy Russell, son of Roscoe Russell, switched that around. He said, "I put pretty wood on the outside where you can see it." The reversal of the bottoms did not negatively affect the sound quality of his instruments as all were very loud and their penetrating tone could be clearly heard in a string band setting. Raymond determined his dulcimers were loud enough without that second bottom and had already stopped using it before I met him in the 1970s. His nephew, Jacob Ray Melton, continued to use the double bottom on his dulcimers. Unfortunately, all of these makers have passed away leaving us to carry on their work of building and playing.

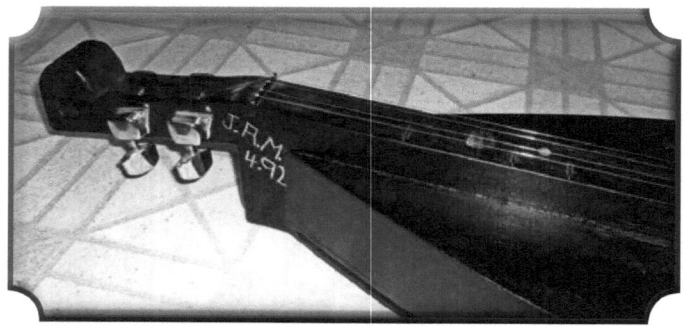

This Jacob Ray Melton dulcimer has a right angle instead of a curve on the lower part of the scroll.

One-Piece Head/Hollow Fretboard/D-Shaped Tailpiece

In all the old Melton-style dulcimers, a long 2" X 4" piece of wood was shaped into a one-piece combined head/fretboard/tailpiece. Jacob Ray Melton told me he put the sides onto the head/fretboard/tailpiece first and then added the top. I drew a sketch as he described it to me.

Frets

All the Melton dulcimers and the other historic Virginia/Galax Dulcimers were constructed using staple frets under the first two strings for noting. Raymond used old round wire ladies' hair pins for his frets, but Jacob Ray used broom wire. When asked how he shaped the wire into staples, Jacob Ray replied, "I bend them around cutting pliers to get them all the same width." Roscoe Russell switched to using frets all the way across in the 1970s, as did his son Roy. This, along with a more modern fret scale, may have been in response to the influence of revivalist building techniques of the period. Raymond and Jacob Ray continued to use staple frets for all of the dulcimers I have seen attributed to them.

Raymond was the only Galax Dulcimer maker I knew who used a 6.5 fret. It became a standard feature on most of his dulcimers around the 1960s. We do not know if he was using it earlier than that or not. I suspect he did because he played in so many bands over the years and would have needed it to survive. To avoid retuning, he carried one dulcimer for D and G tunes and another one for A tunes. The bands could switch keys as often as they liked, and he was always ready.

Raymond Melton made this cherry dulcimer. You see the original staple frets under the two melody strings with the other two strings left unfretted because they are drone strings. Yes, that is a 6.5 fret! You can also see the bottom brace through the sound holes.

The Builders and the Bracing Mystery

Bracing was a topic not open for discussion with these makers of the old "Galaxes" for some reason. Raymond would never discuss it with me. I only got Jacob Ray to give me information shortly before he died. He did not have an unfinished dulcimer in parts to photograph. As a result, I made a sketch of what he described and purchased one of his dulcimers.

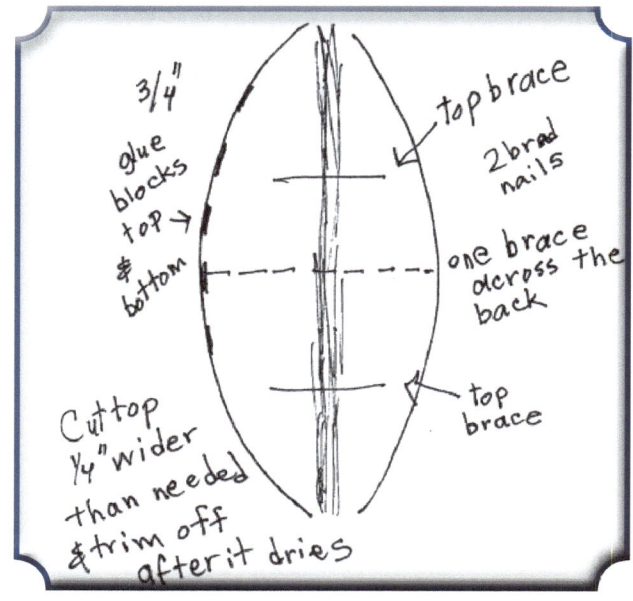

Ben Seymour (www.kudzupatch.net) also met Jacob Ray Melton and purchased one of his dulcimers. Later Ben and I talked about making Galax Dulcimers. I would not let Ben trace or take specific measurements of mine, being true to Raymond and his "secretiveness." We did share ideas and thoughts about construction, so he created the Gaskins/Melton dulcimer model. Ben was determined, and thanks to his initiative and dedication, his accurate construction techniques produced lots of fine Galax Dulcimers. Ben has generously let me use the x-ray images he made of Jacob Ray's dulcimer. You can see the brad tacks and staple frets clearly. (You can find Ben's comments on p. 67.)

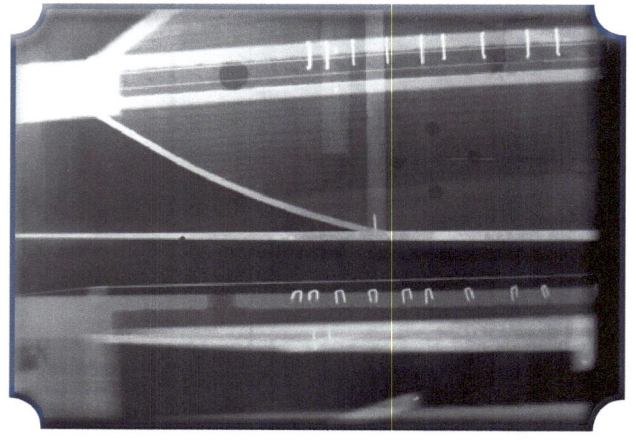

Keith Young, one of the best dulcimer makers in the country (http://appalachiandulcimers.com/appdul.htm) and a good friend of Roscoe Russell, favored the Russell design. Keith worked on one of Roscoe Russell's dulcimers, and while he had it apart, he took photos of the inside bracing. Thanks to Keith for allowing me to share this with you. (You can find Keith's comments and a photo on p. 66.)

Don Neuhauser (Double D Dulcimers, 7914 Hidden River Trace, Charlestown, IN, 47111), a luthier, also makes a Russell-style Galax Dulcimer. His dulcimers differ from the Melton dulcimers with frets all the way across the fretboard and without a 6.5 fret unless requested. The head is a separate guitar-shaped headpiece like the Russells used. Since he used a Roscoe Russell dulcimer for his pattern, he sometimes used the signature concave curve of the Russell dulcimers under the head. These dulcimers are also more tapered at each end. (You can find Don's comments on p. 67.)

Terry Burcham has a dulcimer constructed of poplar wood built by Raymond Melton's older brother, Jacob. More than 80 years old, this instrument still sounds wonderful! When Terry got the dulcimer, it had 3/4" wire staples for frets, some not positioned to produce accurate equal-tempered pitches. Terry replaced all of the frets with banjo fret wire cut like staples to extend under only the first two strings. He also repositioned some of the frets to create a more equal-tempered scale. Terry has graciously shared detailed diagrams of this dulcimer. (You can find Terry's comments and diagrams on p. 69.)

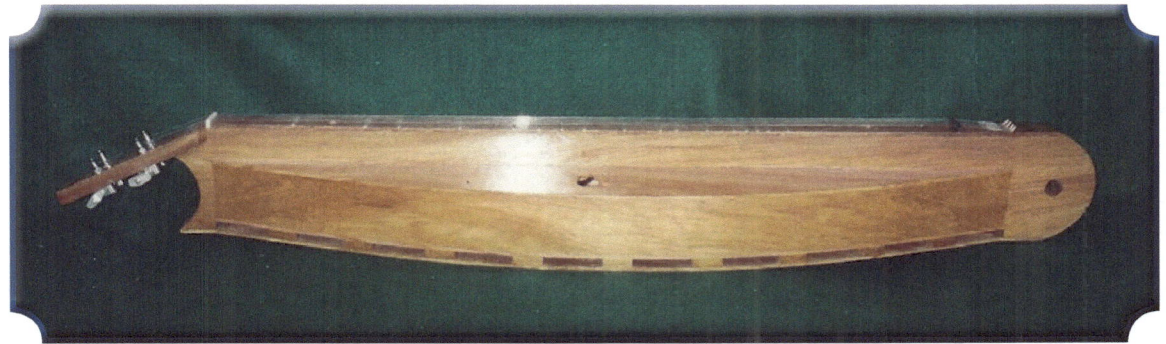

This Roscoe Russell model dulcimer, built by Don Neuhauser and made of curly nara and rosewood, has the signature concave curve under the head.

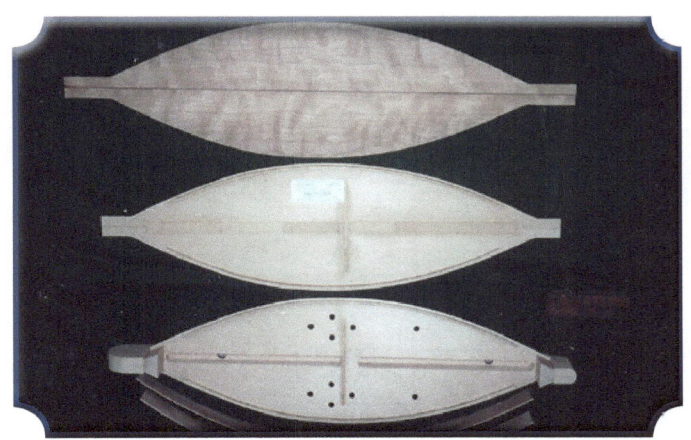

Don Neuhauser provided this photo showing the partially assembled pieces and bracing for one of his Russell-model dulcimers.

Raymond made my chestnut dulcimer from wood taken from an old barn that had been torn down. When he went back to get more, the wood had been burned. That was a lot of good dulcimers gone "up in smoke" - sheitholt for sure!

I have dreamed of making copies of my dulcimer...someday! That someday has now arrived, and I will work with my neighbor Gene Bowlen (http://www.bearcademusic.com/bearcade-music-productions.html) building a few Galax Dulcimers in his workshop. (You can find Gene's comments on p. 70.)

Playing the Galax Dulcimer

The traditional Galax Dulcimer has all four strings of the same gauge and pitch. Raymond Melton always used .010 gauge strings, but I find that using .009 gauge strings on the two drones gives me a lighter drone sound which does not overpower the melody strings. Perfect for the Galax Dulcimer, this string setup works well on other dulcimer body types also.

Noters

- » Noters should be of hard wood, preferably ebony, maple, cherry, or oak.
- » Noters should glide over the strings, rather than be lifted for each individual note.
- » The frets of your dulcimer should ideally be low enough to allow the noter to glide over them without making a "clickity, clackity" sound. If you have this sound when using the noter, have a qualified luthier dress them down for you, being careful to avoid "fret buzz" in the process.

Tuning and Notation

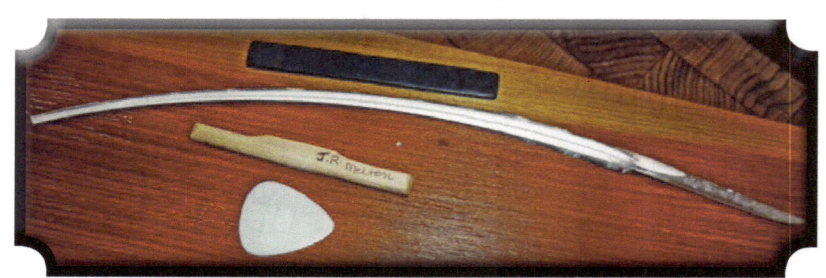

Tune all four strings to D beside middle C on the piano. Numbers in the music notation indicate the fret to be played. Use the noter on the first two strings of your Galax Dulcimer.

Strumming

I learned about strumming arrows from Lois Hornbostel at the first workshop I conducted for her. She suggested I use this technique, and it works GREAT! The arrows indicate the direction I strum, but not always a particular time value.

Use the traditional counting system to interpret the rhythm of each tune. Count each note value like the example below. In cut time, play the tune twice as fast with a two-beat feel instead of a four-beat feel. The 6/8 time tunes will have a two-beat feel.

- ↓ strum in toward your body
- ↑ strum out away from your body
- V̂ strum in, then out
- ∧̬ strum out, then in

13

Holding the Turkey Quill or Pick

Here I strum with a turkey quill. I use the turkey quill only for demonstration purposes because I find in jam sessions and performances, the ends fray and break frequently. I also prefer the sound I get with a pick.

Here I use the pick for strumming. The first two strings are noted, and the other two strings drone. I use Jim Dunlop .46mm picks because they are very flexible, durable, and have less pick "clatter."

Holding the Noter

The traditional way of holding the noter is to press on the end of the noter with your index finger. I place the middle finger beside the noter and against the fretboard to help brace and guide the noter, so I can control it.

Using A Capo

Years ago I figured out by tuning the two drone strings on my Galax Dulcimer with its 6.5 fret up to an E, I could play virtually all "old time A" tunes by starting at the 4th fret. Some folks had started using dowel sticks attached to rubber bands as capos on their dulcimers to change keys. This didn't work on my big, ol' Galax Dulcimer, but I figured if you can change the pitch by pressing the string down, you should be able to change the pitch by lifting the string. I took an old nut, shortened the length, put it under my drones, adjusted the groves in the nut to the correct height, and I had an E drone! I called this creation a "false nut." Using it under my drone strings at the first fret creates ddee. This saves me lots of time (no retuning and no broken strings), and I could easily go from one key to another. I can use this technique for playing Em and E Dorian tunes as well as the old time A Mixolydian and Dorian tunes. (See photo.)

Interestingly, when I came up with this idea, Raymond went home and made one, too. He tried it for a few weeks, then he stopped using it. When I asked him why he stopped using the false nut, he said, "I kept knocking the blame thing out!"

If you use a regular capo, place it at the first fret to change dddd to eeee for the key of A.

Playing D Tunes on the Galax Dulcimer

To play in the key of D on the Galax Dulcimer, tune all of the strings to the D beside of middle C on the piano. The scale will start on the open string. Use the 6+ (6.5) fret for the C#.

Note	D	E	F#	G	A	B	C	C#	D	E	F#	G	A	B	C	D
Fret	0	1	2	3	4	5	6	6+	7	8	9	10	11	12	13	14
Scale	do	re	mi	fa	sol	la		ti	do							

Note the first two strings as your melody strings.

If you do not have a Galax Dulcimer, tune the strings to DAD. Use the same fret numbers as indicated in the music notation.

For many old time tunes, the stress/unstressed notes and the rhythmic bow licks/strumming patterns turn a simple, sparse note pattern into a great dance tune!

Tunes in the Key of D

21. Big Liza Jane
22. Black-Eyed Susie
23. Chapel Hill March
24. Ducks on the Millpond
25. Fortune
26. Green Willis
27. Job of Journey Work
28. Julie Ann Johnson
29. Katy Cline
30. Luther's Walkin' in the Parlor
31. Old Molly Hare
32. Old Time Sally Ann
33. Peek-a-Boo Waltz
34. Sugar Hill
35. Walkin' in the Parlor #1

Jacob Ray Melton made this dulcimer in December of 1991 for Patty Looman, a friend and dulcimer-playing treasure of West Virginia. Jacob Ray wrote his initials on the end piece. I purchased this dulcimer at an auction of some of Patty's instruments.

Big Liza Jane

Tracks 1 - 2

Traditional
arr. Phyllis Gaskins

© 2012 Phyllis Gaskins. All rights reserved.

Just what you needed, another Liza tune! I play this tune in D as notated here. It was played SO well by the brilliant dulcimer player Bonnie Russell, her brother Roy, and her dad Roscoe. Thanks, Bonnie, for this photo of Roy, Roscoe, and you. What a treasure!

Black-Eyed Susie

Tracks 3 - 4

Traditional
arr. Phyllis Gaskins

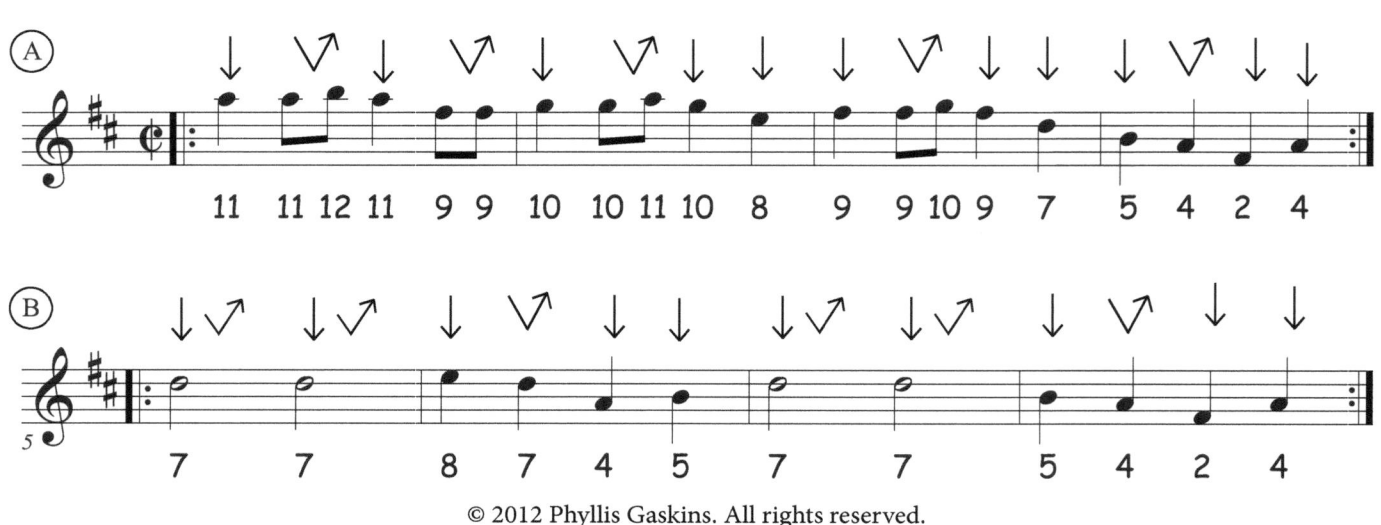

Verses (sung on the repeat of Part A)

Love my wife, and I love my baby,
Love my biscuits sopped in gravy.

Chorus (sung on 1st time through Part B)
Hey, Hey, Black-Eyed Susie!
Hey, Hey , Black-Eyed Susie!

All I want in God's creation
Is a pretty little wife with a big plantation.

Chorus

All I need to make me happy
Is a little bitty baby to call me Pappy.

Chorus

One named Sam and the other one Davy,
One liked ham and the other one gravy.

Chorus

We had wonderful times playing this tune and others with The Blue Sky Ramblers at the Galax Old Fiddler's Convention. Pictured here are Dea Felts (fiddle), Melvin Felts (banjo), Raymond Melton (dulcimer), and two brothers Mumford (Mumps) and Howard Dillon on guitars. What a foot-tapping old time dance band sound they had!

Chapel Hill March

Traditional
arr. Phyllis Gaskins

Track 5

© 2012 Phyllis Gaskins. All rights reserved.

This tune, also called **Chapel Hill Serenade,** survived as one of the few jigs in the mountains of southwest Virginia. It is a Galax variant of the English jig, **The New Rigged Ship**. Luther Davis said the tune was used as a march at the end of the school term for what was known as a "school breaking." At the end of the year, the "scholars" would march two by two out of the school building led by two fiddlers playing this tune. One line would march right and the other left, out and around the building, passing each other in the back of the building, then returning to the front with a shout for the end of the school year. This tune also survived in reel form as **Green Willis**, or **The Raw Recruit**.

Ducks on the Millpond

Traditional
arr. Phyllis Gaskins

Track 6

© 2012 Phyllis Gaskins. All rights reserved.

Ducks on the Millpond, a great old tune, is commonly played in the Galax/Mount Airy region. Emmett Lundy learned the tune from "Old Man" Green Leonard in the latter half of the 19th century. Alan Lomax collected/recorded the tune from Lundy in the late 1930s.

Some lyrics (sung to the Part A)
Ducks on the Millpond,
Geese in the clover;
Tell them pretty girls,
I'm comin' over.

Ducks on the Millpond,
Geese flyin' over,
Stand back pretty girl,
Dance in the clover.

Ducks on the Millpond,
Geese in the ocean,
All them pretty girls
Gettin' in the notion.

Ducks on the Millpond,
Geese on the ocean,
Hug that pretty girl
If I take a notion.

Fortune

Track 7 - 8

Traditional
arr. Phyllis Gaskins

© 2012 Phyllis Gaskins. All rights reserved.

This great old tune is rarely heard outside the Surry County, North Carolina/ southwest Virginia region. The lyrics describe some unfortunate things that can happen to a fellow when he has had too much to drink. The song lyrics were collected in the early 1900s from a broadside (without music) published by L. De Marsan titled **I'll Ne'er Get Drunk Again**. I've never met a Galax/Mount Airy musician who did not play a version of this tune.

Don Neuhauser made this wormy maple and rosewood Galax Dulcimer for his sister, Dot Christenson, who has placed second at the Galax Fiddler's Convention three times and has been among the top ten winners for ten years in a row. (Photo: Dot Neuhauser)

Green Willis

Traditional
arr. Phyllis Gaskins

Tracks 9 - 10

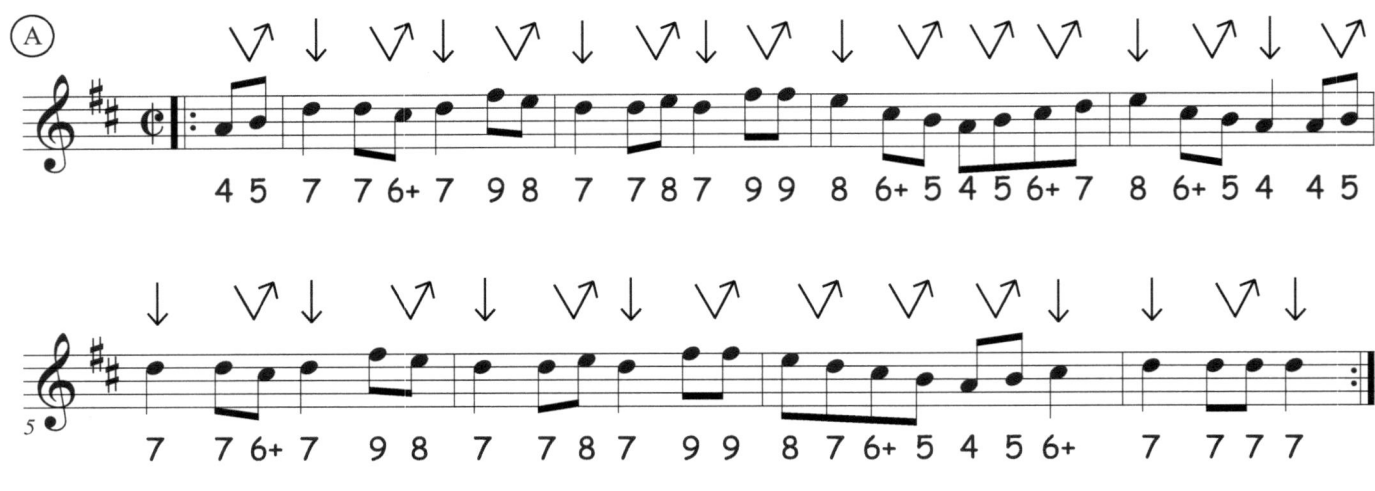

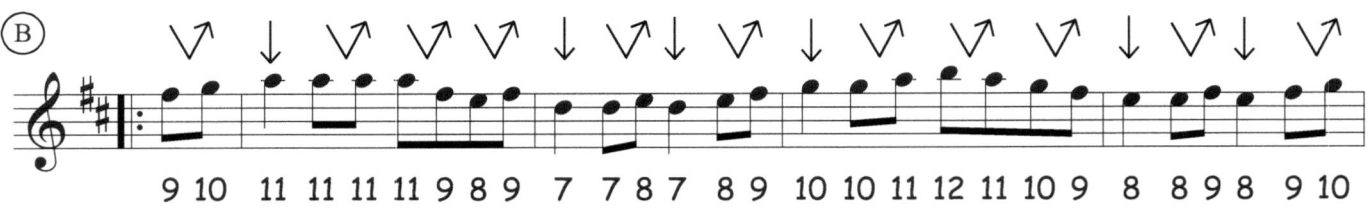

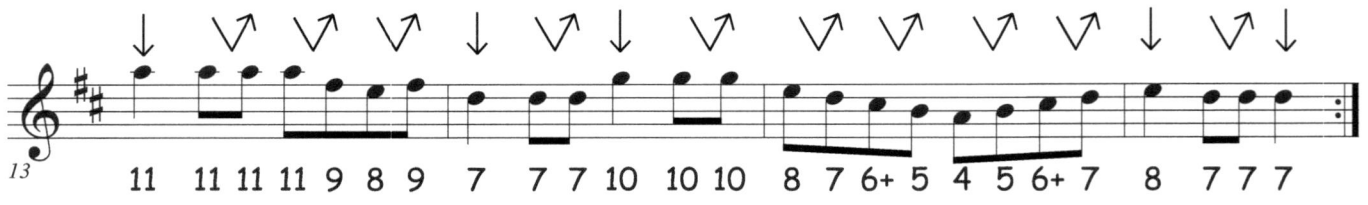

© 2012 Phyllis Gaskins. All rights reserved.

Green Willis, also known as the **Raw Recruit** and **First Come in Was a Bumble Bee**, is a reel version of the tune, **Chapel Hill March (Serenade)**. The famous fiddler Taylor Kimble from Laurel Fork, Carroll County, Virginia, was one of the main sources for the spread of this tune named for Green Willis, a 19th-century fiddler from the Galax area of southwest Virginia. Some humorous lyrics associated with the tune have survived.

Drinkin' moonshine at the age of fifteen,
Caused poor Willis's face to turn green;
Then it turned red 'cause he was ashamed,
So we'll play the tune that goes by the name
Of...Green Willis.

Job of Journey Work

Tracks 11 - 12

Traditional
arr. Phyllis Gaskins

A
9 8   7 4 3 2 3 4 5   6 4 5 3 4   9 8   7 4   3 5 4 2   3 5 4 2 0   2 3

4 4 3 4 2 4 1 4   0 0 0 1 2 1 2 3   4 7   5 6+ 7 8 6+   7   7 6+ 7

B
7 8   9   8 9 10 9 8 9   7   4 3 4   7 8   9   8 9 10 9 8 6+   7   7 6+ 7 8 9 10

11 9 10 8 9 9 8   7 6+ 7 8 9 9 8   7 4 3 2 3 4 5   6 6 5 6 5 6   7 5 6 4 5 3 4 2

3 5 4 2 0 2 3   4 4 3 4 2 4 1 4   0 0 0 1 2 1 2 3   4 7 5 6+ 7 8 6+   7   7 6+ 7

© 2012 Phyllis Gaskins. All rights reserved.

James Morrison (1893-1947), the great Irish fiddler who emigrated to America, recorded **Job of Journey Work**, an Irish set dance tune. Tunes like this were used for specific solo dances; only around a dozen of these tunes still exist. The Part B (12, 14, or 16 bars) is always longer than the Part A (8 or 12 bars). As my "Job of Journey Work," my noter and pick have danced over the Galax Dulcimer strings for many years. Jim and I learned this tune in our blessed journeys through old time, Irish, and Scottish music experiences with the "old masters."

Julie Ann Johnson

Tracks 13 - 14

Traditional
arr. Phyllis Gaskins

© 2012 Phyllis Gaskins. All rights reserved.

Julie Ann Johnson, a local Galax tune, has spread all over the country. We learned it from the recording of Emmett Lundy's fiddle playing done by the Lomaxes for the Library of Congress. That syncopated swing is the hallmark of Galax-style fiddle playing.

Terry Burcham (1992) plays his dulcimer made by Jacob Melton (older brother of Raymond Melton) more than 80 years ago. Terry, a fine Galax Dulcimer player, has been carrying on this traditional dulcimer style for over 35 years. He continues to use the turkey quill for strumming. (Photo: Sara Burcham)

Katy Cline

Traditional
arr. Phyllis Gaskins

Track 15

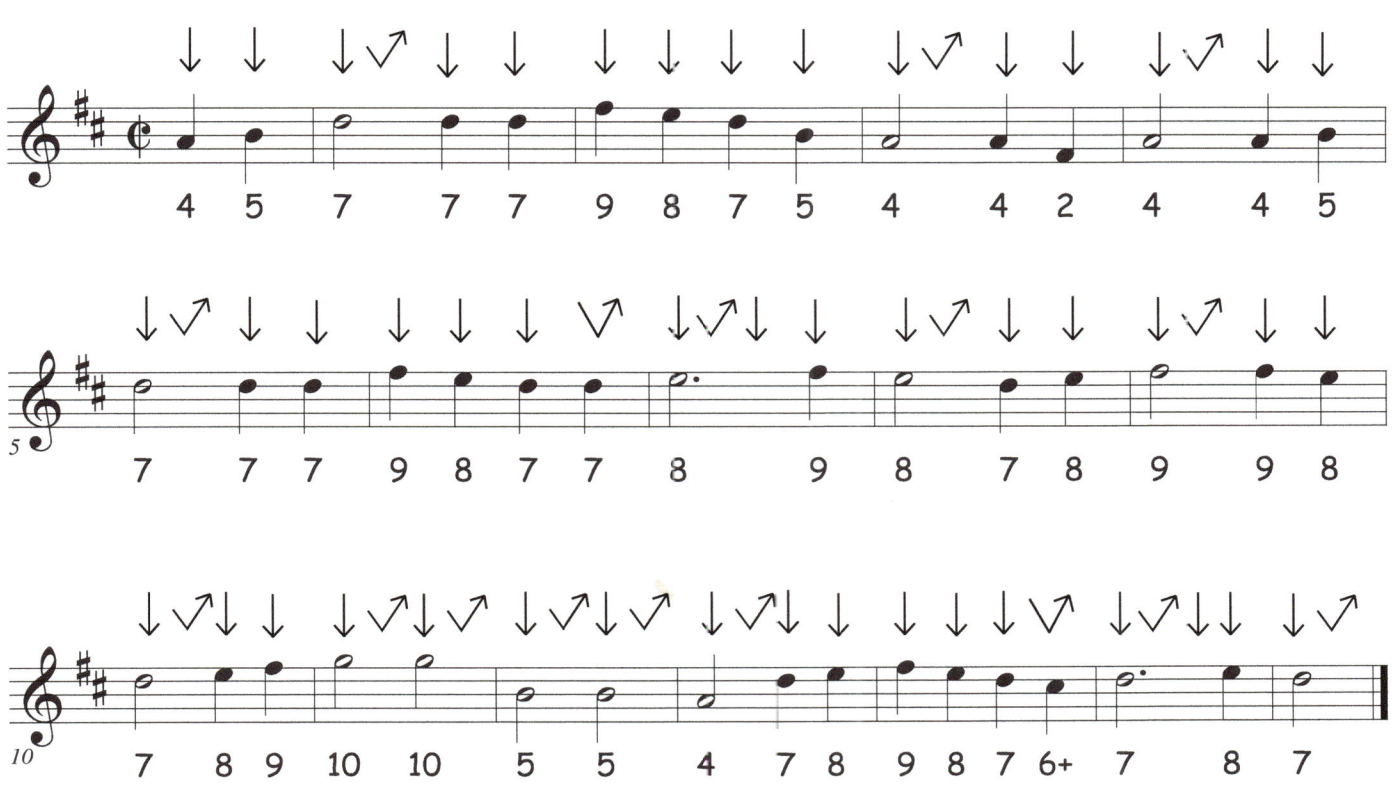

© 2012 Phyllis Gaskins. All rights reserved.

Katy Cline, a common tune in the southwest Virginia/northwestern North Carolina region, exemplifies popular music being absorbed and becoming entrenched in traditional culture. It is an adaptation of a popular song **Kitty Clyde** written and composed by L. V. H. Crosby and published in 1853. I am fortunate to have an original broadside of the song from that period.

Chorus (as sung in Southwest Virginia)
Oh, say that you love me Katy Cline, Katy Cline.
Oh, say that you love me darlin' do.
Oh, say that you'll be my own true love,
Oh, say that you love me, Katy Cline.

Blue O'Connell, my apprentice in the 2010-2011 Virginia Folklife Apprenticeship program, performs in concert with her Galax Dulcimer. Her dulcimer was made by Clarence Roberts of Galax, who made one or two of these dulcimers at my request in the 1980s. Blue, a multi-talented deaf musician, has a cochlear implant. Blue gave me the incentive to forge ahead in my dream of creating this book. (Photo: Candace Schoner)

Luther's Walkin' in the Parlor

Traditional
arr. Phyllis Gaskins

Tracks 16 - 17

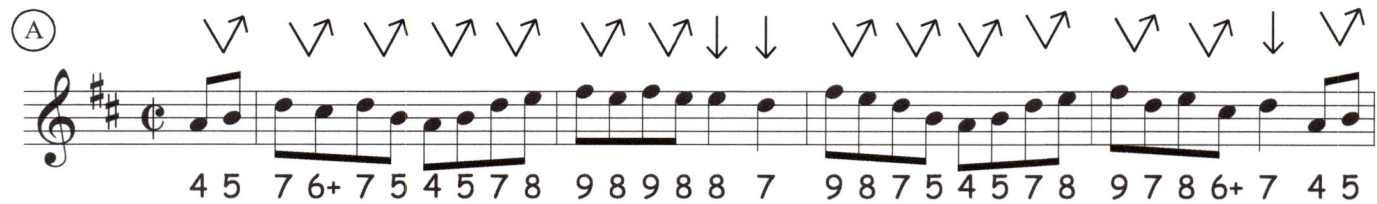
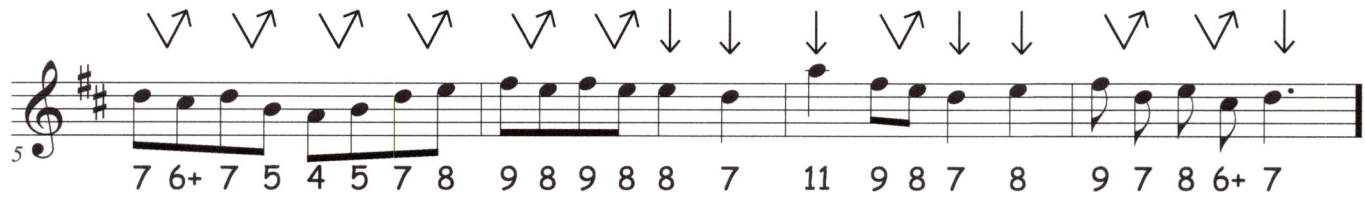
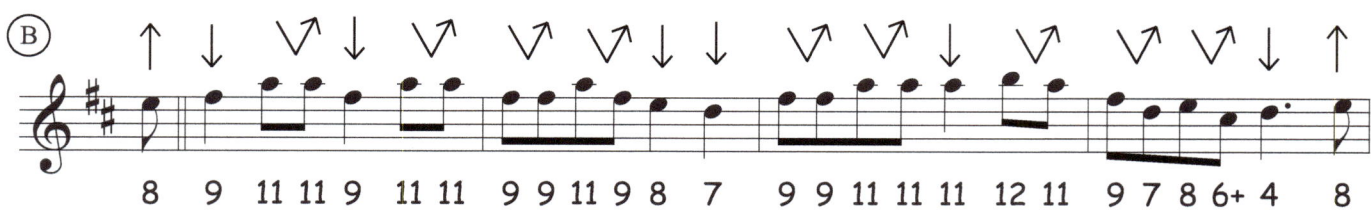
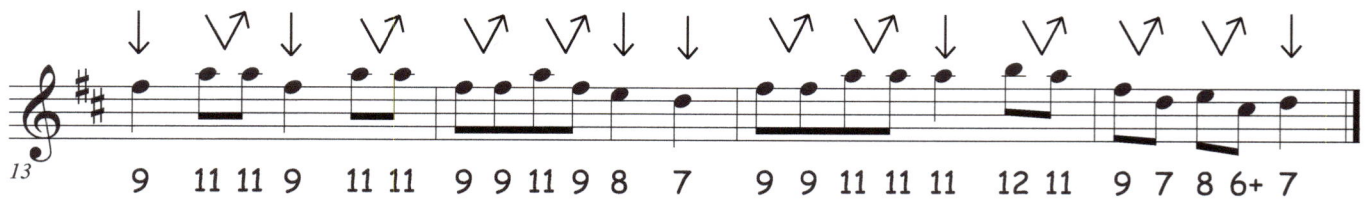

© 2012 Phyllis Gaskins. All rights reserved.

Our friend, Galax fiddler Luther Davis (1887 - 1986), was 92 in August 1980 when the photo at the right was taken. My husband, Jim, had just won 2nd place fiddle at The Galax Fiddler's Convention playing this tune which he had learned from Luther. Luther learned this tune from local fiddle legend, Uncle Charlie Higgins (1878 - 1967). On this day when we shared the ribbon with Luther, he said, "I didn't win, but I had a horse that did."

Old Molly Hare

Tracks 18 - 19

Traditional
arr. Phyllis Gaskins

Old Molly Hare, an Appalachian variant of the Scottish tune **The Fairy Reel**, is a lively dance tune with lots of lyrics and was one of the first old time tunes I learned to play.

Lyrics (sung to Part A)
Old Molly Hare,
Whatcha doin' there?
Runnin' though the cotton patch
As hard as I can tear.

Leg like a deer,
Foot like a bear,
Runnin' through the cotton patch
As hard as I can tear.

Old Molly Hare
Yonder comes a bear,
Comin' down the hill
As hard as he can tear.

Old Molly Hare,
Whatcha doin' there?
Sittin' on the hillside
Lookin' at the bear.

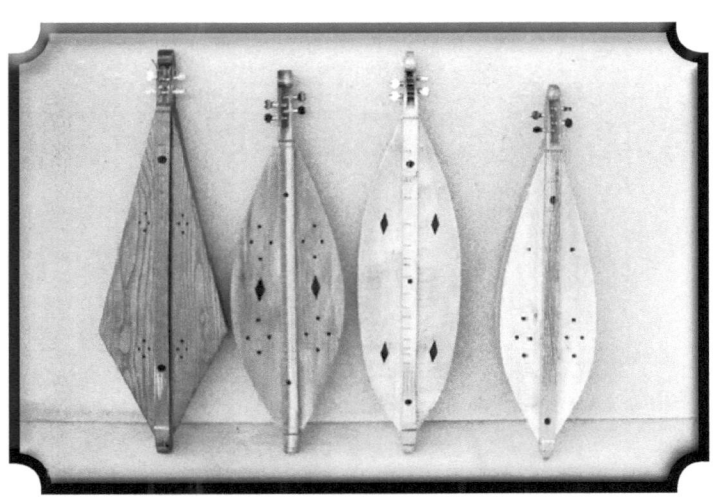

Four Raymond Melton dulcimers from 1971-72 show varying sizes, shapes, and sound hole patterns.
(Photo: Terry Burcham)

Old Time Sally Ann

Traditional
arr. Phyllis Gaskins

Tracks 20 - 21

(Play # 14, 14, 14 on the second time through the A part.)

© 2012 Phyllis Gaskins. All rights reserved.

Old Time Sally Ann, a "big tune" from southwest Virginia and northwestern North Carolina (especially around Galax and Mount Airy), is known by virtually every old time musician in this region. The floating lyrics nearly always sung with this tune (but other tunes as well) imply "adult content" and are rarely sung in mixed company. A "high D" is often used in the repeat of Part A in the three places indicated.

Peek-a-Boo Waltz

Traditional
arr. Phyllis Gaskins

Track 22

© 2012 Phyllis Gaskins. All rights reserved.

I learned this great waltz from Luther Davis. Found in many different fiddling traditions throughout the United States and Canada, it is especially well known in western and southwestern Virginia. Nothing is known of the composer, but the tune was first published in 1881 by William J. Scanlon (1856-1898), a popular vaudeville singer.

Sugar Hill

Tracks 23 - 24

Traditional
arr. Phyllis Gaskins

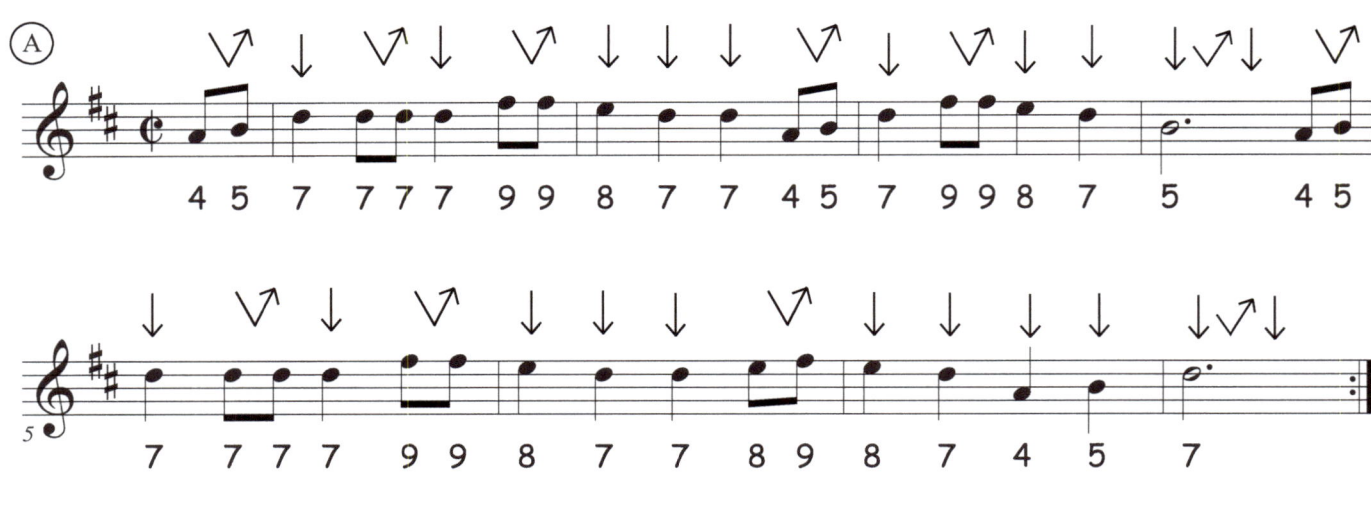

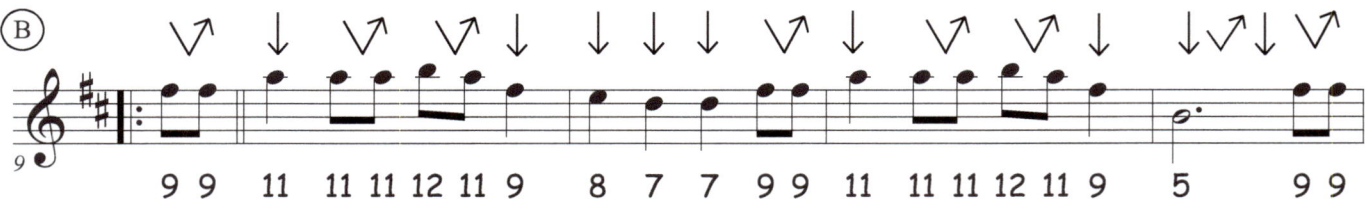

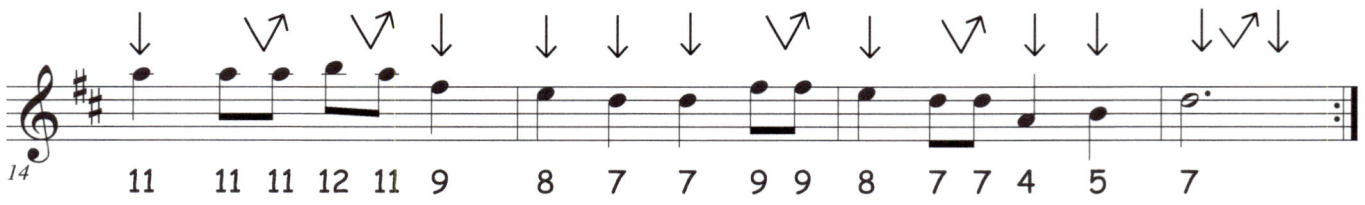

© 2012 Phyllis Gaskins. All rights reserved.

One drizzly Saturday morning at a fiddler's convention near Princeton, West Virginia, Giles Lephew sat with me on the tailgate of our pickup truck with only the topper door protecting us from the wet. On that morning Giles worked patiently phrase by phrase on the banjo with me repeating the phrases on the dulcimer until I learned to play this tune. At the next fiddler's convention, I placed third playing it.

Walkin' in the Parlor #1

Tracks 25 - 26

Traditional
arr. Phyllis Gaskins

© 2012 Phyllis Gaskins. All rights reserved.

We call this **Walkin' in the Parlor #1** because it is the first **Walkin' in the Parlor** we learned. I remember The Roan Mountain Hilltoppers playing this one in their campsite at a fiddler's convention in Dublin, Virginia. At that time they would alternate the two Part A's starting with the high Part A the first time and the low Part A the second time around. The words I remember are, "I saw Sal walkin' in the parlor, Walkin' in the parlor late last night."

Jim and I have loved the music of the Roan Mountain Hilltoppers from Carter County, Tennessee, since we first met them in 1977 at a fiddler's convention in Chilhowie, Virginia. Pictured band members are Creede Birchfield on banjo (then 72), Joe Birchfield on fiddle (then 65), and Joe's son, Bill, on guitar. Bill told me he plays both guitar and banjo "upside down and backwards." Today he plays fiddle in the band and his wife, Janice, plays washtub bass as they carry on this family's tradition.

Playing G Tunes on the Galax Dulcimer

To play in the key of G on the Galax Dulcimer, tune all of the strings to the D beside of middle C on the piano. The scale will start on the third fret. Use the 6th fret for the C natural.

Note	D	E	F#	G	A	B	C	C#	D	E	F#	G	A	B	C	D
Fret	0	1	2	3	4	5	6	6+	7	8	9	10	11	12	13	14
Scale				do	re	mi	fa		so	la	ti	do				

Note the first two strings as your melody strings.

If you do not have a Galax Dulcimer, tune the strings to DGD. Use the same fret numbers as indicated in the music notation.

Tunes in the Key of G

37. Dance All Night with a Bottle in Your Hand
38. Did You Ever See the Devil, Uncle Joe?
39. Ebenezer
40. Evening Star Waltz
41. The Girl I Left Behind Me
42. John Brown's March
43. Long Journey Home
44. Merriweather
45. Sandy River Belle
46. Seneca Square Dance
47. Silly Bill
48. Unclouded Day

Notice the interesting head on a very rare Raymond Melton dulcimer I purchased in an antique shop. Made around 1970-71, it might be a creative experiment or a special request. This dulcimer is the only one I have ever seen with staple frets all the way across the fretboard. It does have the 6.5 fret and is made of cherry and poplar.

Dance All Night with a Bottle in Your Hand

Tracks 27 - 28

Traditional
arr. Phyllis Gaskins

A

5 6 | 7 7 7 7 8 7 6 | 5 4 3 3 3 | 5 5 4 2 0 2 4 6 5 4 | 5 4 3 3 3 | 5 6

(10) When you repeat the tune hit the high G (10) instead of the D (7) note.

7 7 7 7 8 7 6 | 5 4 3 3 3 5 5 | 4 2 0 2 4 4 6 4 | 5 4 3 3 3 5 6 | 5 4 3 3 3 8 9

B

10 10 10 10 9 10 11 | 12 11 12 13 12 10 10 | 11 10 11 12 11 9 9 | 10 9 10 11 10 7 9 | 10 10 10 10 9 10 11

12 11 12 13 12 11 10 | 14 14 14 8 9 9 | 10 10 10 10 8 9 | *D.S.* 10 10 10 10 8 9 | *Last Time* 10 10 10 10

© 2012 Phyllis Gaskins. All rights reserved.

Jacob Ray Melton, nephew of Raymond Melton, and I played this tune, a favorite of his, together on the day we drew the sketches of his dulcimer design (p. 15-16). I purchased this dulcimer from him on that same day.

Did You Ever See the Devil, Uncle Joe?

Tracks 29 - 30

Traditional
arr. Phyllis Gaskins

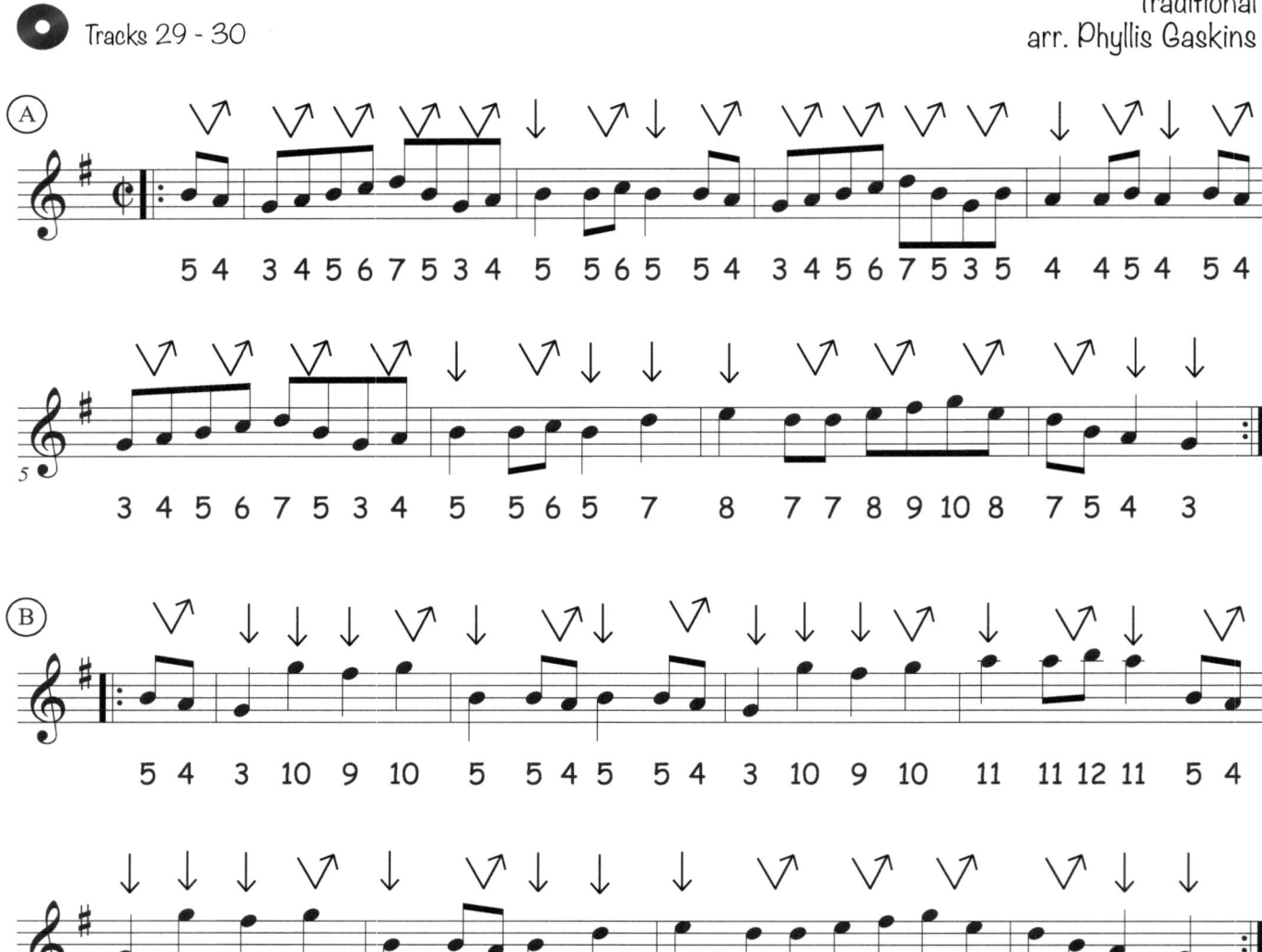

© 2012 Phyllis Gaskins. All rights reserved.

Did You Ever See the Devil, Uncle Joe? (**Hop Light [High] Ladies**) is a widely known tune throughout the United States. Outside the Appalachians it is known as **Mrs. (Miss) McLeods (MacLeods) Reel**. The tune, originally from Scotland, was collected around 1800 on the Isle of Skye by the great Scottish traditional composer, Niel Gow (1727-1807), with the original title, **Mrs. MacLeod of Raasay's Reel**.

Verses (Part A)
Did you ever see the devil, Uncle Joe, Uncle Joe, (3x)
Don't mind the weather if the wind don't blow.
Did you ever go to meetin', Uncle Joe, Uncle Joe, (3x)
Don't mind the weather…

Does your horse carry double, Uncle Joe, Uncle Joe, (3x)
Don't mind the weather…

Chorus (Part B)
Hop light ladies, three in a row.
Hop light ladies, cake's all dough.
Hop light ladies, three in a row.
Don't mind the weather if the wind don't blow.

Ebenezer

Tracks 31-32

Traditional
arr. Phyllis Gaskins

A
5 6 7 5 4 3 4 5 6 7 5 4 3 4 5 6 7 10 9 9 10 11 9 11 4 5

6 4 3 2 3 4 5 6 4 3 2 3 4 5 7 7 5 4 2 3

B
7 8 10 9 9 10 11 12 7 8 10 9 9 10 11 12 9 10

11 12 12 11 11 9 10 11 12 12 11 11 9 8 7 7 5 4 2 3

© 2012 Phyllis Gaskins. All rights reserved.

An all-time favorite at dulcimer contests in Southwest Virginia, I bet this tune was played on every one of these dulcimers made from 1971-1972 by Raymond Melton. Look at the many shapes, sizes, and sound hole patterns. For these nine dulcimers, different woods were used: from left to right, chestnut and ash; all maple; all cedar; poplar and locust; sugar maple and ash; cherry and ash; sugar maple and ash; all walnut; plywood and cedar. (Photo and information: Terry Burcham)

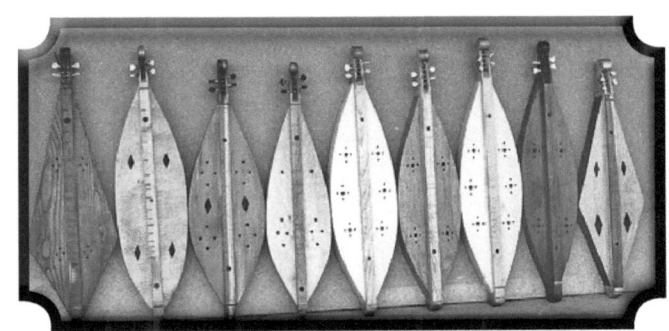

Evening Star Waltz

Traditional
arr. Phyllis Gaskins

Track 33

© 2012 Phyllis Gaskins. All rights reserved.

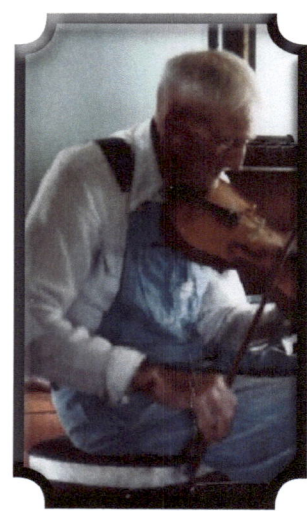

This tune exemplifies how light classical art music can filter down and be absorbed, modified, and simplified through aural transmission in traditional culture. The parent tune is a beautiful multiple-part waltz written by Viennese composer Joseph Lanner (1801-1843). It appears in **The Peter Beemer Manuscript**, a handwritten collection of tunes played for dances in Warren's Diggins, Idaho, in the 1860s. The Beemer transcription is complex and in multiple parts like the original. Jim and I learned this version from our dear friend and mentor, Luther Davis (pictured here), who said he had gotten it from "this girl" (never named) he played dances with when he was young and working in rural Illinois. He may be the local Galax source because Luther's neighbor Emmett Lundy played the tune as well. Ben Jarrell (Tommy's dad) also played and recorded this tune with Da Costa Woltz's Southern Broadcasters. Unlike other versions, this version is not "square" (evenly measured for the caller to make the dance work) or in two keys.

The Girl I Left Behind Me

Tracks 34 - 35

Traditional
arr. Phyllis Gaskins

© 2012 Phyllis Gaskins. All rights reserved.

The Girl I Left Behind Me, extremely popular during both the Revolutionary War and the Civil War and known in nearly all fiddling traditions, has a long history going back in the British Isles and Ireland to the 1600s. Its ancestors include the Irish song, **An Spailpin Fanach,** and the English tune, **Brighton Camp**. An Appalachian variant called **Peggy Walker Blues** appeared in early recordings by Dock Boggs among others.

Jim and I have played this longtime favorite of ours for Civil War period programs and reenactments, especially in our local village of Port Republic, one of the major battle sites of Stonewall Jackson's Valley Campaign.

John Brown's March

Traditional
arr. Phyllis Gaskins

Track 36

© 2012 Phyllis Gaskins. All rights reserved.

Numerous tunes make reference to history's famous abolitionist, John Brown. While the origin of this particular tune is unclear, it has been attributed by some to Missouri and western Virginia.

On this Jacob Ray Melton dulcimer made in 1992 for Patty Looman, you can see the spacers separating the two bottoms.

37

Long Journey Home

Track 37

Traditional
arr. Phyllis Gaskins

© 2012 Phyllis Gaskins. All rights reserved.

Traditional Lyrics
Lost all my money but a two dollar bill,
Two dollar bill, boys, two dollar bill.
Lost all my money but a two dollar bill,
I'm on my long journey home.

Cloudy in the West and it looks like rain,
Looks like rain, boys, looks like rain.
Cloudy in the West and it looks like rain,
I'm on my long journey home.

Black smoke a-risin' and it surely is a train,
Surely is a train, boys, surely is a train,
Black smoke a-risin' and it surely is a train,
I'm on my long journey home.

Startin' into rainin' and I gotta go home,
I gotta go home, boys, I gotta go home,
Startin' into rainin' and I gotta go home,
I'm on my long journey home.

I can still hear Jacob Ray Melton playing this tune during dulcimer week at Appalachian State University in 1992. Thanks, Diane Gravlin, for this photo of me with Jacob Ray Melton.

Merriweather

Tracks 38 - 39

Traditional
arr. Phyllis Gaskins

© 2012 Phyllis Gaskins. All rights reserved.

Jim and I learned this in 1978 from the Malcolm Dalglish and Grey Larsen LP entitled **The First of Autumn**. We recorded it on our first cassette tape in 1986. I love to play this tune! I recently discovered the well-known fiddler, Bruce Greene, had collected this tune in 1973 from W. L. "Jake" Phelps who lived in or near the town of Elkton in Todd County, Kentucky. I had assumed the tune was a Northern tune, but Greene found it in Kentucky. It may have been named after a prosperous farmer who lived in that area. Researchers have made some connections with the person who may have composed the tune and Merriweather's daughter.

Sandy River Belle

Tracks 40 - 41

Traditional
arr. Phyllis Gaskins

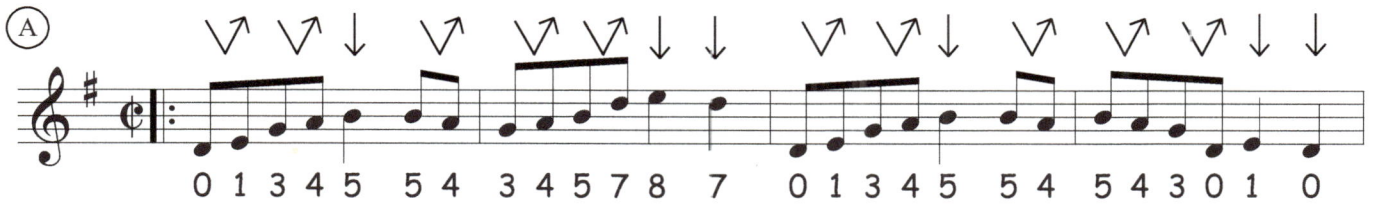

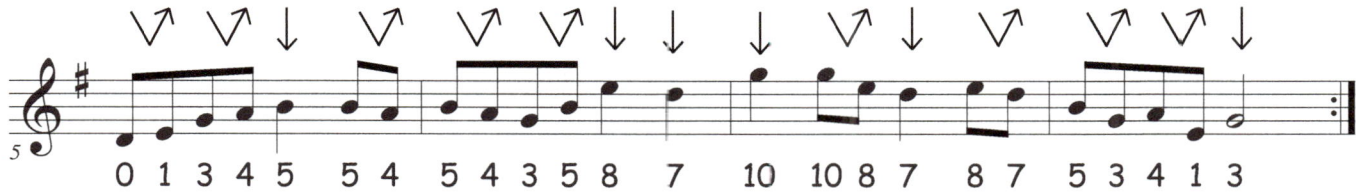

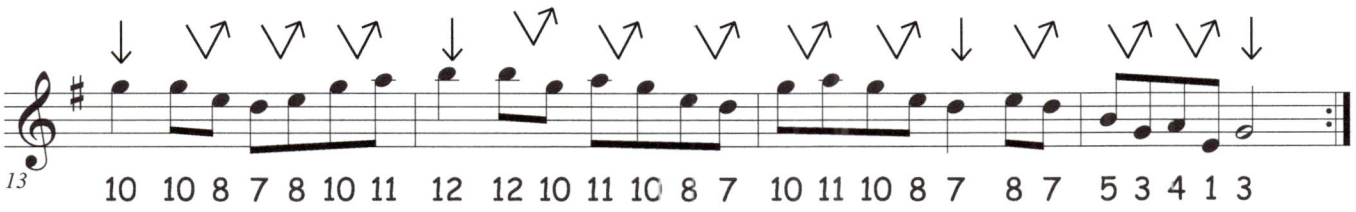

© 2012 Phyllis Gaskins. All rights reserved.

One of several tunes bearing this name, the title most likely refers to the area of the Big Sandy River which marks the border between West Virginia and Kentucky. The tune is particularly widespread and very popular throughout southwest Virginia. The Port Road String Band (Gene Bowlen, banjo; Mike Harrison, guitar; Jim Gaskins, fiddle; Pat Harrison, bass; and yours truly with my Melton dulcimer) loves to play this tune for dances.

Seneca Square Dance

Traditional
arr. Phyllis Gaskins

Tracks 42 - 43

© 2012 Phyllis Gaskins. All rights reserved.

Seneca Square Dance, a great fiddle tune from the Civil War era, is found in the repertoires of most old time musicians throughout the entire United States, but most likely came from the area around Seneca, Missouri. The tune illustrates the common phenomenon that many traditional tunes have multiple titles. The most common alternate title for this tune is **Waiting for the Federals**. Another title is **Shelby's Mules** (a reference to Confederate cavalry Gen. Joseph Orville "JO" Shelby). Other less common titles include **Little Home to Go To** and **Higher Up the Monkey Climbs**.

Silly Bill

Tracks 44 - 45

Traditional
arr. Phyllis Gaskins

One of Raymond Melton's favorites, this tune quickly became one of my favorites as well. In my mind I can still see and hear him. I would ask, "What's the name of that tune?" He would smile a wide grin, lean back in his chair as far as he could without tipping over, throw back his head, shake it side to side, and say, "Sil-l-ly Bill." The words would rattle out of his mouth because he was shaking his head so much! I would ask him every time I heard him play this tune, and every time the answer was the same. This photo of Raymond was taken in the early 1970s. (Photo: Terry Burcham)

© 2012 Phyllis Gaskins. All rights reserved.

Unclouded Day

Tracks 46 - 47

Traditional
arr. Phyllis Gaskins

Unclouded Day, a hymn piece, popular as a dance tune among Grayson and Carroll County musicians in southwest Virginia, was composed by an Adventist minister, Rev. J.K. Alwood (1828-1909). Traveling home one day in Ohio, he witnessed a beautiful rainbow against a dense, black nimbus cloud. He was so stunned and spiritually inspired by the sight he created this lovely song. This was a favorite of Raymond Melton seen jamming in this photo of The Blue Sky Ramblers.

© 2012 Phyllis Gaskins. All rights reserved.

Playing A / A-Modal Tunes on the Galax Dulcimer

Tunes in this section may be in A major or any of the old time A-Modal keys; therefore, key signatures vary. To play these A tunes on the Galax Dulcimer, tune all of the strings to the D beside middle C on the piano. Then either capo or use the false nut at the first fret to change the drones. The scale will start on the 4th fret. In some tunes you will use fret 6 for the C natural, in some tunes the 6+ (6.5) fret for the C#, and some tunes require both.

Note	D	E	F#	G	A	B	C	C#	D	E	F#	G	A	B	C	D
Fret	0	1	2	3	4	5	6	6+	7	8	9	10	11	12	13	14
Scale					do	re	meh	mi	fa	sol	la	teh	do	re	meh	fa

Note the first two strings as your melody strings.

If you do not have a Galax Dulcimer, tune the strings to DGD. Place a capo at the first fret and use the same fret numbers as indicated in the music notation. If you have a capo across all of your strings at the first fret, the number 1 in the music notation is an open strum.

Tunes in the Key of A/A-Modal

50. Breakin' Up Christmas
51. Cluck Ol' Hen
52. Cold Frosty Morning
53. Dinah
54. Falls of Richmond
55. Highlander's Farewell
56. Kitchen Girl

57. New Castle (Texas)
58. Sail Away Ladies
59. Sally Goodin
60. Sheep Shell Corn
61. Sugar in the Gourd
62. Train on the Island

My cherry dulcimer made by Raymond Melton has its original tuners. It was refretted by Keith Young. I use .012 gauge strings on it and keep it tuned to C for playing in the keys of C, F, and Dm.

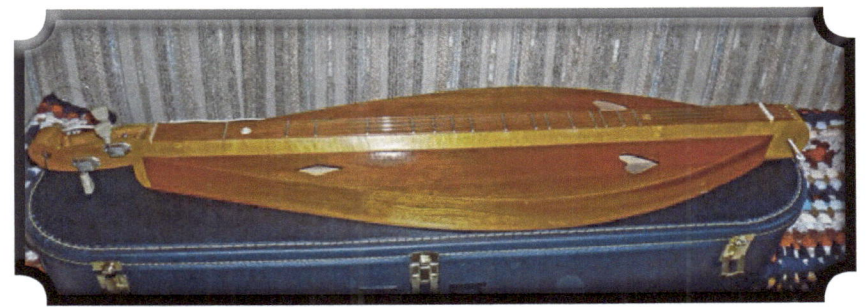

Breakin' Up Christmas

Tracks 48 - 49

Traditional
arr. Phyllis Gaskins

© 2012 Phyllis Gaskins. All rights reserved.

In one of our many visits to his home, Luther Davis told us the story of when he was young and folks would celebrate the 12 days of Christmas by visiting each others' homes. The folks would travel from house to house and have nightly suppers, music, dancing, and singing until the 12 days/nights were over. They called this "breakin' up Christmas."

Some Lyrics (sung to Part A)
Sanny Claus come, done and gone,
Breakin' up Christmas right along.

Way back yonder, long time ago,
The old folks danced the dosey-do.

Hooray Jack and hooray John,
Breakin' up Christmas right along.

Jim and Luther play a tune together. When we were learning tunes from Luther, we would ask if we had it right yet. He would often reply, "No, you've not got that tune just right yet." And so we stayed longer until we had it "just right."

Cluck Ol' Hen

Tracks 50 - 51

Traditional
arr. Phyllis Gaskins

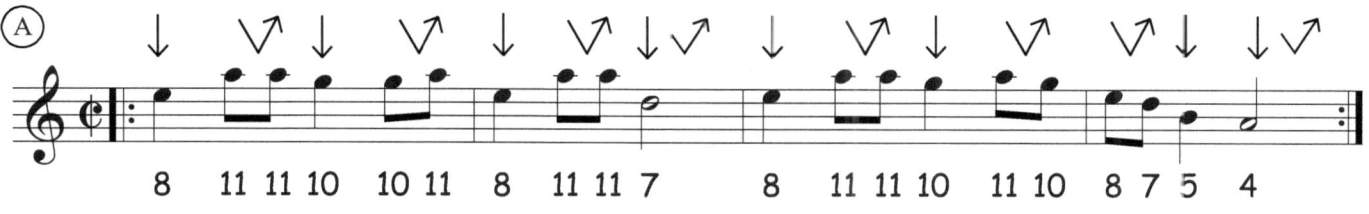

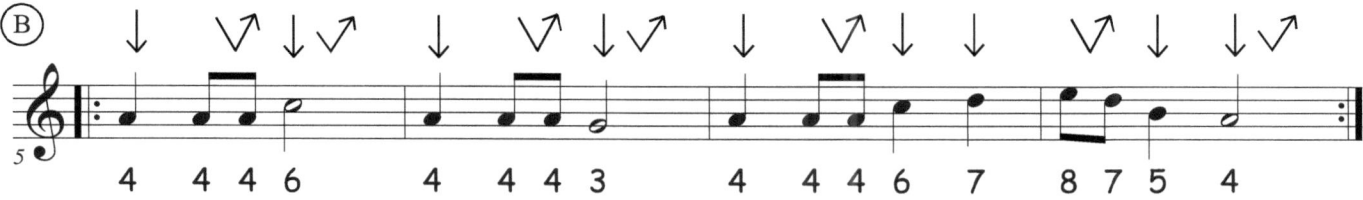

© 2012 Phyllis Gaskins. All rights reserved.

Chorus (Part B)
Cluck ol' hen, cluck I said,
Cluck ol' hen, your widdies are dead.

Verses (Part A)
My ol' hen is a good ol' hen,
She lays eggs for the railroad men,
Sometimes one, sometimes two,
But that's enough for the whole dang crew.

My ol' hen is a good ol' hen,
She lays eggs for the railroad men,
Sometimes eight, sometimes ten,
But that's enough for the railroad men.

Had an ol' hen and she had a wooden leg,
Best dern hen that ever laid an egg.
She laid more eggs than any hen around the barn.
Another little drink wouldn't do me any harm.

Had an ol' hen, she cackled and she flew,
If I'd a-been a rooster, I'd a-flew too.

Last Chorus
Cluck ol' hen, cluck in the lot.
The next time you cluck,
You'll cluck in the pot!

Our friend Luther Davis told us in the Galax area baby chickens were called "widdies."

Below you see a picture of Bonnie Russell when she was a child playing in the yard. That's her pet chicken, Mack, on her shoulder. Bonnie said he loved the sound of the dulcimer!

Cold Frosty Morning

Tracks 52 - 53

Traditional
arr. Phyllis Gaskins

A
1 0 1 3 4   4 3   4 3 4 5 6 8   0 1   3 4 5   4 3 4 5   4   3 4 5 6 7

1 0 1 3 4   4 3   4 3 4 5 6 8   4 4   6 5 4 6 5   4 3 5   4   5 4

B
8 9 11   11   11 12 11 10 8   7   8   9   10 9 8 10   9 8 7 9 8

4   6   7   8   6 5 4 6 5   4 3 5   4   5 4

© 2012 Phyllis Gaskins. All rights reserved.

Cold Frosty Morning, a wonderful old tune, comes primarily from the fiddle playing of Henry Reed. Alan Jabbour collected it from Reed and brought it to widespread popularity through the highly influential recording of it with his band, the Hollow Rock String Band, in the late 1960s. We used it for our band name, Frosty Morning.

Frosty Morning included Karen and Mel Lee on mandolin and guitar with Jim and me on fiddle and dulcimer.

Dinah

Traditional
arr. Phyllis Gaskins

Tracks 54 - 55

© 2012 Phyllis Gaskins. All rights reserved.

No, this is not **Someone's in the Kitchen with Dinah** or **Aunt Dinah's Quilting Party**…Dinah must have been a popular gal, as a lot of tunes float around with her name attached to them. I love to play this tune. I have no idea where we learned it, but I do remember shortly after we learned it, we taught it to Giles Lephew who was playing in our fiddler's convention band, the Elk Run String Band. He liked it so well we decided to play it right then and there in competition at the Galax Old Fiddler's Convention. We didn't win, but we got recorded on the album that year, more rewarding than a ribbon!

Falls of Richmond

Traditional
arr. Phyllis Gaskins

Falls of Richmond, an old tune, comes from the fiddle playing of the highly influential West Virginia fiddler, Edden Hammons (1876-1955). In the late 1800s, he had the reputation as one of central West Virginia's finest fiddlers. His music was collected in field recordings in 1947.

Highlander's Farewell

Traditional
arr. Phyllis Gaskins

Tracks 57 - 58

© 2012 Phyllis Gaskins. All rights reserved.

We learned this tune from the playing of Luther Davis and Emmett Lundy (1864-1953). Lundy, Luther's neighbor, had done field recordings for the Library of Congress. **Highlander's Farewell** goes back to the "Old Country." It laments the sad departures of the Highlanders and the Lowlanders bidding each other farewell as the Highlanders left Scotland. Emmett Lundy learned this tune from the playing of "Old Man Green Leonard" (1810-1892), a renowned fiddler of the Galax region.

Music is often attached to the land. Just up the path, past Luther's garden, and over a fence or two was Emmett Lundy's land.

Kitchen Girl

Tracks 59 - 60

Traditional
arr. Phyllis Gaskins

© 2012 Phyllis Gaskins. All rights reserved.

Kitchen Girl, a great old Virginia fiddle tune, has been extremely popular throughout the country since the late 1960s due to the highly important field work done by Alan Jabbour. He collected the tune from the great Virginia fiddler, Henry Reed, who had a treasure trove of rare, beautiful fiddle tunes.

This old wood cookstove was in Luther Davis's kitchen. He cooked us up some fine beans, cabbage, and biscuits on this old stove. Mmmm...good!

51

New Castle (Texas)

Traditional
arr. Phyllis Gaskins

Tracks 61 - 62

New Castle (Texas), another rare, crooked tune (one with a nonstandard number of beats/measures) comes from Henry Reed, the great Giles County, Virginia, fiddler. This one was also collected by Alan Jabbour. The old fiddlers had so many tunes that, in their later years, the rarer and less frequently played tunes sometimes had their names lost or temporarily forgotten. Such was the case with this tune. When first collected, Reed could not remember the exact name, so he called it **Texas** because he had picked it up from a fiddler from Texas. On a subsequent visit, Reed informed Jabbour the correct name, **New Castle**, had come to him. New Castle is the county seat of neighboring Craig County.

Sail Away, Ladies

Traditional
arr. Phyllis Gaskins

Tracks 63 - 64

© 2012 Phyllis Gaskins. All rights reserved.

Numerous fiddle tunes/fiddle songs have this title. Common from Virginia and North Carolina through central Kentucky and middle Tennessee in different versions, this tune has floating lyrics that appear in other members of the "Sally Ann" tune family: **Sally Ann**; **Sail Away, Ladies**; and **Great Big Taters in Sandy Land**. We like to sing these lyrics with the chorus sung on Part A and the verses sung on Part B. We usually begin and end this tune on Part A unless we are playing for a dance.

Chorus
Don't you rock 'im die-de-o, (3x)
Sail away, ladies, sail away!

Verses
I've got a home in Tennessee,
Sail away, ladies, sail away!
That's the place I wanna be,
Sail away, ladies, sail away!

Come along, boys, and go with me,
Sail away, ladies, sail away!
We'll go back to Tennessee,
Sail away, ladies, sail away!

When I get my new house done,
Sail away, ladies, sail away!
I'll give my old one to my son,
Sail away, ladies, sail away!

Sally Goodin

Tracks 65 - 66

Traditional
arr. Phyllis Gaskins

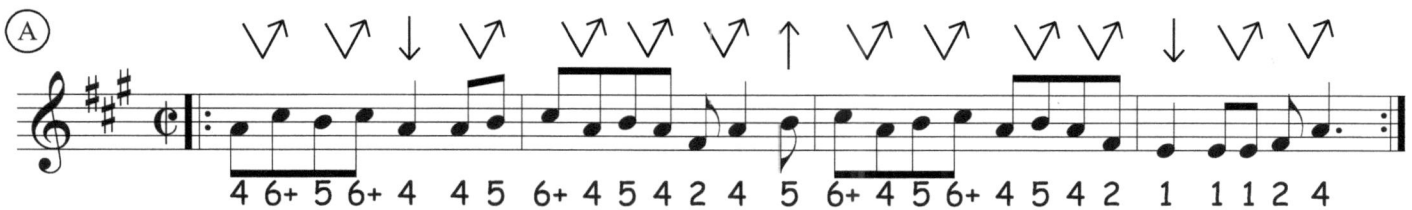

© 2012 Phyllis Gaskins. All rights reserved.

Sally Goodin (Goodwin), a widely known breakdown and play party song/tune typically in the key of A, comes from the upland South. While a staple in many fiddlers' repertoires, especially in Kentucky, it is not universally known and played throughout the country. It has, however, become a major tune in the Texas fiddle tradition, thanks to the burgeoning recording industry. Recorded (released) by the great Texas fiddler Eck Robertson, with 13 variations in 1923, it became a "Number 1" country hit. With 13 variations from Robertson, you can see why we have so many differing melodies and choices of keys. Fiddlers in southwest Virginia traditionally play this tune in the key of G.

Sally Goodin (G)

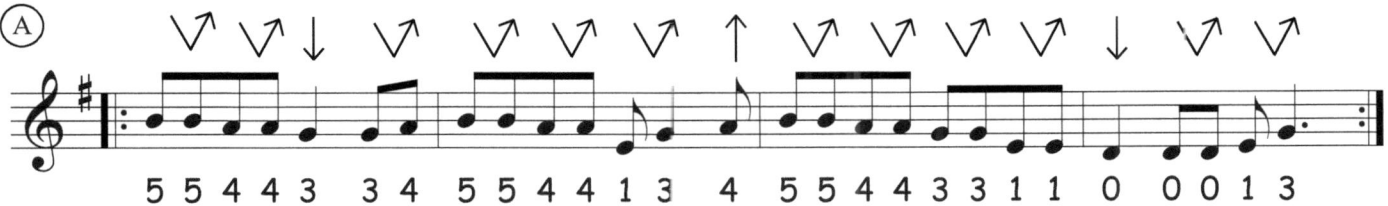

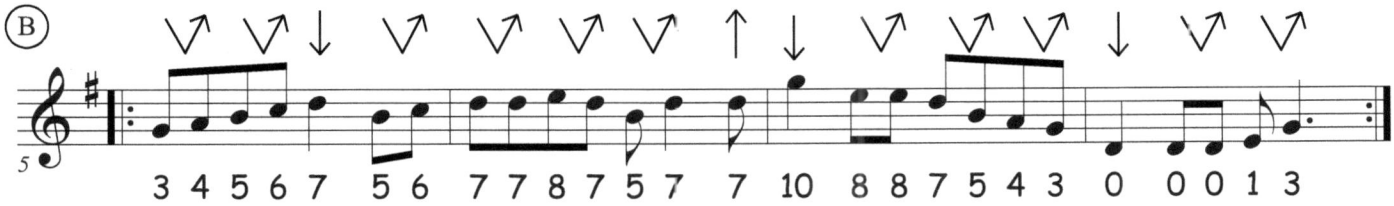

© 2012 Phyllis Gaskins. All rights reserved.

Sheep Shell Corn

Traditional
arr. Phyllis Gaskins

Tracks 69 - 70

© 2012 Phyllis Gaskins. All rights reserved.

When I play this tune, I see the old buck sheep rubbing his horn up and down an ear of dried corn (shelling corn) to get the kernels off, so he can eat 'em! This tune is specifically associated with the Galax area fiddlers, especially Emmett Lundy, but is rarely heard in other traditional areas. This particular melody has a set of lyrics even rarer than the fiddle tune itself. Fiddle tunes with lyrics are often referred to as fiddle songs. Numerous songs from the Ozarks and African American sources have the same title, but are sung to different melodies.

Some lyrics I sing to Part A
Never seen the like since I been born,
Sheep shell corn by the rattlin' of his horn!
Corn's in the cupboard and butter's in the churn,
Never seen the like since I been born!

Sheep shell corn by the rattlin' of his horn,
Send to the mill by the whippoorwill.
Take care gents and let me through,
I'm gonna dance with little Mollie Lou.

Sheep shell corn by the rattlin' of his horn,
Never seen the like since I been born.

Sugar in the Gourd

Traditional
arr. Phyllis Gaskins

Tracks 71 - 72

© 2012 Phyllis Gaskins. All rights reserved.

I have both heard and watched Bonnie Russell play **Sugar in the Gourd** many times. I was always amazed at how skillfully and clearly she noted this one! Thanks, Bonnie, for this photo of you and your dad, Roscoe.

Like so many tunes rooted in the southern African American tradition, this one became grounded in the music traditions of the mountain folks.

Chorus
Sugar in the Gourd and you can't get it out,
Way to get the sugar is to roll the gourd about.

Lyrics
Met her down the road, she danced on a board,
The wind from her shoes knocked Sugar in the Gourd.
Sugar in the gourd and the gourd upon the ground,
Only way to get the sugar is to roll the gourd around.

Some folks say that a preacher won't steal,
But I caught one in my cornfield.
He had a bushel and his wife had a peck,
The baby had a roastin' ear hung around his neck.

I went down in the old corn field,
A blacksnake grabbed me by the heel.
I turned 'round and did my best,
Then drove my head in a hornet's nest.

Train on the Island

Traditional
arr. Phyllis Gaskins

Track 73

© 2012 Phyllis Gaskins. All rights reserved.

Known by virtually every fiddler in the Galax area of southwest Virginia and the Surry County area of North Carolina, **Train on the Island** is a "driving" old dance tune in the key of A (in AEAE cross tuning on the fiddle). A favorite of our mentor Luther Davis, the tune came to wider prominence through the playing and recording of the well known Carroll County, Virginia, fiddler, Norman Edmonds (1889-1976). We have played this fiddle song version for years.

Some lyrics
(Part A)
Train on the Island, don't you hear it blow?
Go tell my true love, I'm sick and I can't go,
(Part B)
Sick and I can't go, love, sick and I can't go.

(Part A)
Yonder comes my true love, how d'ya think I know?
Tell her by th' apron strings, tied in a double bow,
(Part B)
Tied in a double bow, love, tied in a double bow.

(Part A)
Train on the Island, don't you hear it squeal?
Go tell my true love, how happy I do feel,
(Part B)
How happy I do feel, love, how happy I do feel.

Playing Two-Key Tunes on the Galax Dulcimer

Tunes in this section are in two keys: either G for Part A and D for Part B or D for Part A and G for Part B. Tune all of the strings to the D beside of middle C on the piano. The scale for the G section will start on the third fret; use the 6th fret for the C natural. The scale for the D section will start on the open string; use the 6+ (6.5) fret for the C#.

Note	D	E	F#	G	A	B	C	C#	D	E	F#	G	A	B	C	D
Fret	0	1	2	3	4	5	6	6+	7	8	9	10	11	12	13	14
G Scale				do	re	mi	fa		sol	la	ti	do				
D Scale	do	re	mi	fa	sol	la		ti	do							

Note the first two strings as your melody strings.

If you do not have a Galax Dulcimer, tune all of your strings to D. The bass string will be an octave lower, creating "bagpipe" tuning. Tuned this way, use the music as written.

Or if you do not have a Galax Dulcimer, tune to DGD. Use fingerings on the other strings to create a suitable drone on the middle string(s), or use chords on the part for which your dulcimer is not tuned. Play the G part in the DGD tuning, and use chords for the D part.

Simple chords for the D part could be:

G   D   A

Tunes in Two Keys

64. Flop-Eared Mule

65. Jenny Lind Polka

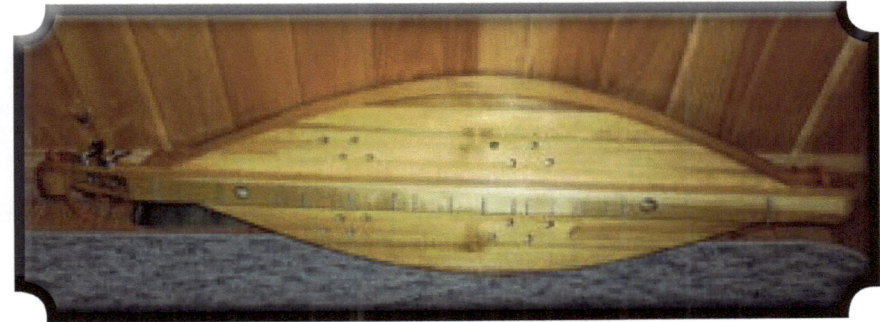

I like the traditional sound hole pattern on this poplar dulcimer made by Jacob Ray Melton. He used regular fret wire cut to fit under only the first two strings.

Flop-Eared Mule

Tracks 74 - 75

Traditional
arr. Phyllis Gaskins

[Sheet music with tablature numbers:]

(A) 10 11 12 10 7 8 7 5 5 4 6 5 4 3 4 5 6 7 10

12 10 7 8 7 5 5 4 6 5 4 3

(B) 2 3 4 4 4 5 4 4 4 1 3 3 2 1 1 0 1 2 3 4 2

4 4 4 5 4 4 4 1 3 3 2 1 1 0

© 2012 Phyllis Gaskins. All rights reserved.

Flop-Eared Mule has been a fiddler's convention staple for years, and many dulcimer players have gotten first place with this tune including my friend, Gin Burris. Gin started playing the dulcimer in the early summer of 1978. She learned this tune from Sylvan White in 1979 and says, "It took me about 5 minutes to learn." She plays everything by ear. Thanks, Gin and Joey, for this photo. Gin is pictured here with her Roscoe Russell dulcimer, made in the early 1970s.

Jenny Lind Polka

Tracks 76 - 77

Traditional
arr. Phyllis Gaskins

[Sheet music notation]

© 2012 Phyllis Gaskins. All rights reserved.

Jenny Lind is a polka in form and not at all common in the Appalachians. Here we have another example of art music piercing the skin of traditional culture. The tune is named after the "Swedish Nightingale," opera singer Jenny Lind, born in 1820. She toured the United States and was wildly popular from big cities to small hamlets. Our dear friend and fellow musician, Ivry Kimble, told me once after I played the tune for her that her dad, Taylor Kimble, had also played the tune. We, unfortunately, never heard him play it, and he left no recording of it. I am not sure how close the two versions might be. Here we are with Ivry after playing "The Merry-Go-Round" WPAQ radio show in Mt. Airy, North Carolina.

Roscoe Russell Galax Dulcimer and Keith Young Early Virginia Model

by Keith Young (1929 - 2012)

I became acquainted with Roscoe Russell on my trips to the Fiddler's Convention in Galax, Virginia, in the 1970s. As a dulcimer maker, I was intrigued with the tremendous sound that came out of the dulcimers he and others from the Galax area made at that time. I had the good fortune to repair one of Roscoe's dulcimers and had to remove the back. While I had it apart, I took some pictures of Roscoe's "secret bracing."

Roscoe used a one-piece Douglas fir 2 x 4 for the fret board/head block/tail block. He hollowed out below the fret board and fastened sides in slots made in the head block and tail block. (See picture.) The top is very thin (1/16") sheet of veneer used in making plywood. It has very little strength on its own and needs bracing to strengthen and stiffen it. The back is of the same veneer and well braced for strength. An additional back of 3/32" Luan plywood is fastened to the veneer back by many 1/4" x 1" blocks around the edge to suspend the dulcimer 1/4" above the double back. It works in much the same way a resonator works on a banjo.

I build my Early Virginia Model a little differently. I use a separate headblock and tailblock that is not a part of the fretboard. I resaw my own wood for the top and back to my own specifications (a little less than 1/8" depending on the density of the wood). I brace the back and top only if the wood is too thin to be strong or stiff enough to hold flat without bowing or caving. I hollow out the fretboard and put soundholes in the fretboard as well as in the top, similar to some of the oldest dulcimers found along the Great Philadelphia Wagon Road of the 1700s and still used in the Galax area. I also use steel tuning pins to emulate the iron tuning pins that some of the earliest makers made in their own blacksmith shop. I use modern fret wire for the frets or optional wire cleats used before the modern fret wire was widely available. I also use four strings of the same gauge (.012") tuned to the same note which we now refer to as Galax tuning.

Ben Seymour as Galax Builder

Ben Seymour's first exposure to Galax-style Dulcimers came from hearing Phyllis Gaskins play the instrument in an old-time music performance at a dulcimer festival. He then had an opportunity to view dulcimer historian Ralph Lee Smith's rare collection of instruments including the Galax. Ben began his first Galax after hearing Jacob Ray Melton of Galax, Virginia, the last traditional builder of that dulcimer style, had passed away.

Wanting to preserve the Galax from disappearing from dulcimer history, he decided to add it to his line of modern instruments. In building the first Galaxes, he carefully reproduced Galax features by studying original instruments as well as photographs in Ralph Lee Smith's preeminent history of the dulcimer, **Appalachian Dulcimer Traditions**. When shown one of Ben's Galaxes, Ralph Lee Smith stated Ben had achieved the "traditional-style instrument of the Virginia type."

Ben intends to continue producing Galaxes along with his own style of dulcimer, as he takes seriously his role in preserving the Appalachian heritage of the Galax Dulcimer in particular and the mountain dulcimer in general. He is devoted to carrying the instrument and its story far into America's new century.

Ben custom-made this solid chestnut dulcimer for me. I am so grateful to have it to play. Sounds wonderful, Ben!

An Interview with Don Neuhauser, Maker of a Roscoe Russell Model Galax Dulcimer

PG: Where and when did you first learn about Galax Dulcimers?

DN: In 1977 I went to a festival at Glasgow, near Richmond, Virginia, and met a fiddler, Harold Hausenfluck, and a dulcimer player, Sharon Shelbourne. (Sharon is another top notch Galax Dulcimer player.) We then travelled to the Old Galax Fiddler's Convention where we camped back under the trees in the far corner of the grounds near the old stables. Our campsite was right next to the Bill Burcham, Gin Burris's uncle. (Gin has won many first place ribbons in dulcimer competitions in Southwest Virginia.) At that campsite I met Roscoe Russell, Bonnie Russell, Terry Burcham, and Gin Burris. All of these were accomplished dulcimer players, but I was interested in playing the banjo. A few years later I met Phyllis Gaskins and Alan Freeman there at the fiddler's convention where we jammed together. I was still playing the banjo at that time. In the 1980s we still camped under that same grove of trees, and that is where I met David Snauffer. I became good friends with all of these folks. I was still playing the banjo.

PG: When did your musical interest turn to dulcimers?

DN: I retired and between 1994 - 1996 I joined a dulcimer club and played banjo with them. I started looking at the dulcimers and decided, "I can make a better one than that!" I examined some of Bill Taylor's finely made dulcimers and spent some time in his shop. Around 1996 I bought one of Bill's dulcimers. I also met Warren May in Berea, Kentucky, and visited his shop.

I also spent some time with Bob Mize. I spent two days working in his workshop learning to make dulcimers from him. I cooked and he showed me how to make dulcimers.

I first started making "regular" dulcimers for my family members - kids and grandkids. Then I started selling them. I made a customized left-handed dulcimer for John Renwick, and he won at the Galax Fiddler's Convention with it. He played **Squirrel Heads and Gravy**. I've made over 300 dulcimers now, and 30 of them have been Galax Dulcimers.

PG: When did you first start making Galax Dulcimers?

DN: In 1980 I started camping with the Burrises every year at the Galax Fiddler's Convention, so I got to know them really well. At some point Gin needed some work done on the dulcimer Roscoe had made for her, and she asked me to repair it. She let me use that dulcimer as a pattern for making some. I made Gin one and gave it to her. She called it "Roscoe Don" after me and Roscoe. She won first place with it in 1999 and gave me the ribbon! Then Bonnie (Russell) wanted one, so I made her one, too.

On the day he received it, David Snauffer (in his office) plays his new Galax Dulcimer Don had made for him. In the lower left corner you also see a Tennessee music box, a huge box with dulcimer strings, fretboard, and sound holes. Don got the Tennesse music box pattern from David.

Thanks, Don, for letting me talk you out of this gorgeous chestnut dulcimer when I was at the Great River Road Festival in 2003; it looks and sounds great!

Terry Burcham's Jacob Melton Dulcimer

Terry made these diagrams of his Jacob Melton dulcimer. (Jacob Melton was Raymond Melton's older brother, not to be confused with Jacob Ray Melton, the nephew named for Jacob and Raymond, his uncles.) Terry has been playing this dulcimer since the early 1970s. Terry made highly detailed construction drawings of the dulcimer. The precision measurement details of this more than 80-year-old dulcimer "speak volumes" about the construction techniques employed in the old Galax Dulcimers. Thanks, Terry, for sharing these valuable drawings.

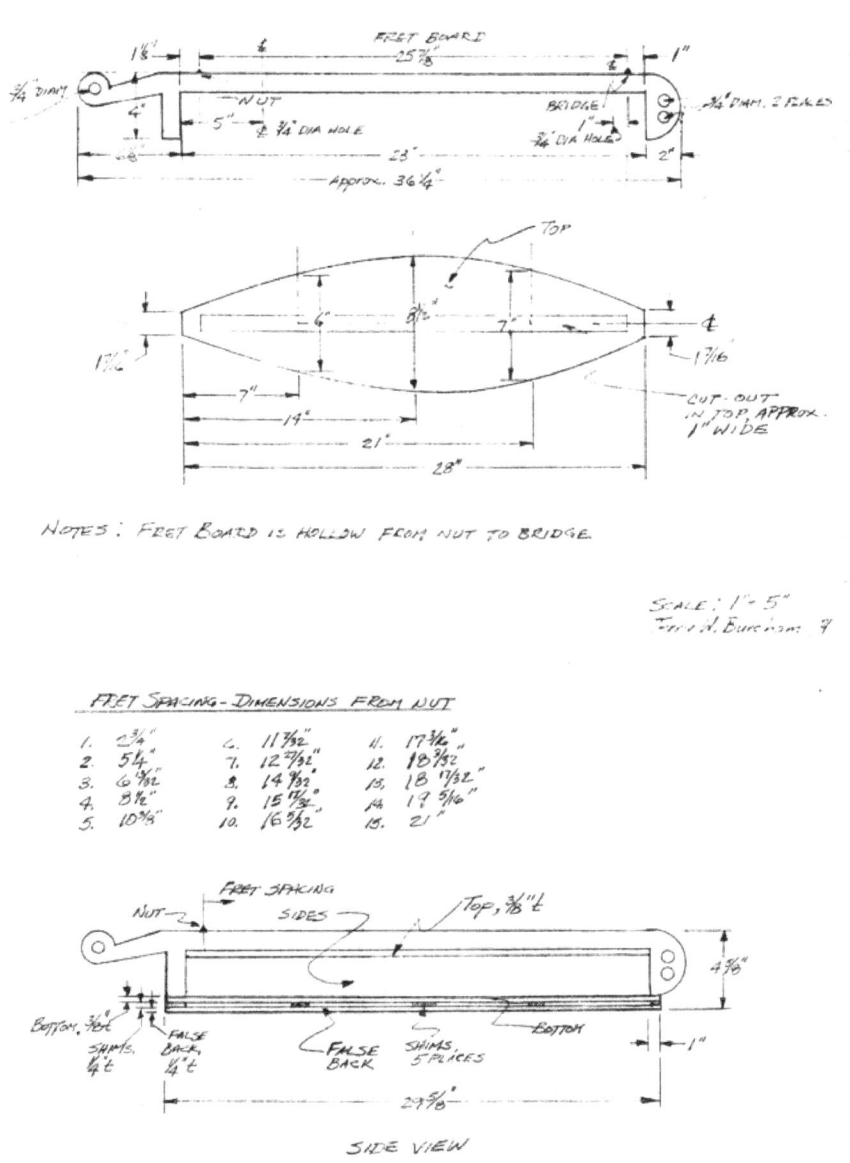

Raymond V. Melton Patterned Galax Dulcimers by Bowlen and Gaskins

by Gene Bowlen

I've had the immense pleasure of playing in bands with Phyllis Gaskins since 1996. During those years we have worked hard to make my clawhammer banjo sound blend together with her dulcimer playing and Jim's fiddle playing. We have talked about the history of the Galax Dulcimer, the Meltons, and how the dulcimer fits into the old-time band.

Phyllis and I have talked about making dulcimers using her favorite instrument made by Raymond Melton as the pattern. We have thoroughly inspected her chestnut model both inside and outside. We have also inspected other instruments made by Raymond Melton as well as the dulcimers of several other makers. Our intention is to duplicate the dimensions, construction techniques, surface finishes, and wood types of these instruments. They will be crafted in the BeARcade Music Productions Woodshop. By using the information we have collected, the instruments we make will have the sound, tone, and volume made famous by the Melton family. (You can learn more about the BeARcade Music Production Woodshop and our dulcimers at http://www.bearcademusic.com.)

Highlander String Band (from left to right) members Allen and Suzanne Kennedy, Phyllis and Jim Gaskins, and Gene Bowlen enjoy making music "just for the FUN of it!" (Photo: Chris Bowlen)

Recordings by Phyllis Gaskins

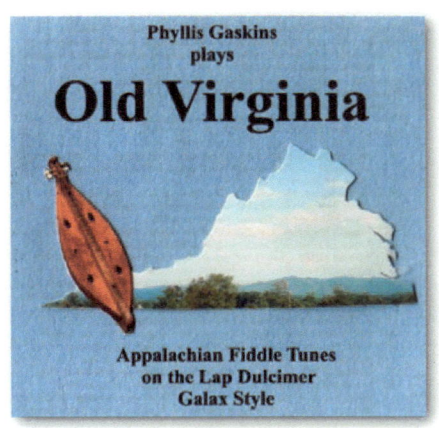

Available from
Shen Fine Music, a division of
Beatin' Path Publications, LLC
302 East College Street
Bridgewater, Virginia 22812
beatinpath@mac.com
Or online at
www.virginiadulcimer.com

DEDICATION

To the Memory of

Raymond Melton

Maker and Player of the
"Old Time Melton Dulcimer"
(dubbed Galax Dulcimer because of its connection
with the Galax area of Virginia and the Galax Fiddler's Convention)

Raymond plays the dulcimer he made for me.

ACKNOWLEDGEMENTS

THANKS to

- » Jim, my husband, without whom I would never have played a dulcimer. I needed his musical expertise and support to get the notes right!
- » Lois Hornbostel, for her unrelenting, positive reinforcement over the many years of sharing and pickin' tunes and for the idea to use arrows to indicate strumming.
- » Karen Holl for her fine editing skills and moral support.
- » Brent Holl for encouragement and teaching me the skills I needed to do the music notation.
- » the many friends and students who have shared tunes with me in jam sessions and social gatherings.
- » You, Lord, for ALL.

About the Author

Phyllis Gaskins, nee Williams, was born in 1947 at home in the midst of a late winter blizzard at the foot of the Blue Ridge just down from the Skyline Drive. She was raised in a family steeped in the struggles and privations of mountain culture. Some of her fondest memories center around sitting on the front porch with her grandmother singing the old folk songs and hymns. Phyllis grew up with a fertile interest in music. She played piano for the choir at the little Bear Lithia Baptist Church just down the road and shared her music with family and friends.

Shortly after college and marriage, Phyllis discovered the mountain dulcimer. Her first one was built from a kit, and she used it for playing in church. While going through a succession of instruments by Bob Mize, Audrey Hash Miller, and herself, she discovered the old Virginia instruments and playing style of Raymond Melton. That was the beginning of her journey to becoming the foremost exponent of the Galax style of playing. She learned at the feet of her master and mentor, Raymond Melton. It wasn't

(Photo: Jim Gaskins)

long before she became a journeyman following in the footsteps of the tradition bearers who preceded her, playing the old tunes in the old style. She was tenacious in her unrelenting focus on her journeywork. She refused to be dissuaded by contemporary, revivalist playing styles, though she admired them a great deal. After a long, productive period of journeywork and the passing of her master, she has become the acknowledged master of the old Galax style and has served in that capacity for many years now.

As a master of the style and as a master teacher, she has spent more than two decades sharing her skill and passing on her knowledge of the dulcimer and traditional music to many others around the country. She has had a colorful and illustrative journey which shows no signs of abating. An important milestone on that journey is the publishing of this book in which she has synthesized much of her vast knowledge about the Galax Dulcimer: its history, construction, builders, playing style, and the beautiful traditional tunes sung to life and renewed with every stroke of pick or quill.

Contributors

Keith Young
Ben Seymour
Jim Gaskins
Don Neuhauser
Gene Bowlen
Terry Burcham
Wilfried Ulrich
Charlie Shaeff

Photos

Don and Dot Neuhauser
Melvin and Dea Felts
Wilfried Ulrich
Early Photography
Gin and Joey Burris
Diane Gravlin
Candace Schoner
Dot Christenson

Steve Zapton
Terry Burcham
Bonnie Russell
Jim Gaskins
Phyllis Gaskins
Chris Bowlen

Track List

Each tune is played slowly one time on the first cut with no repeats of Parts A and B. The second cut of each tune is more up tempo with the tune played as written in the book.

D Tunes
1. Big Liza Jane
2. Big Liza Jane
3. Black-Eyed Susie
4. Black-Eyed Susie
5. Chapel Hill March
6. Ducks on the Millpond
7. Fortune
8. Fortune
9. Green Willis
10. Green Willis
11. Job of Journey Work
12. Job of Journey Work
13. Julie Ann Johnson
14. Julie Ann Johnson
15. Katy Cline
16. Luther's Walkin' in the Parlor
17. Luther's Walkin' in the Parlor
18. Old Molly Hare
19. Old Molly Hare
20. Old Time Sally Ann
21. Old Time Sally Ann
22. Peek-a-Boo Waltz
23. Sugar Hill
24. Sugar Hill
25. Walkin' in the Parlor #1
26. Walkin' in the Parlor #1

G Tunes
27. Dance All Night with a Bottle in Your Hand
28. Dance All Night with a Bottle in Your Hand
29. Did You Ever See the Devil, Uncle Joe?
30. Did You Ever See the Devil, Uncle Joe?
31. Ebenezer
32. Ebenezer
33. Evening Star Waltz
34. The Girl I Left Behind Me
35. The Girl I Left Behind Me
36. John Brown's March
37. Long Journey Home
38. Merriweather
39. Merriweather
40. Sandy River Belle
41. Sandy River Belle
42. Seneca Square Dance
43. Seneca Square Dance
44. Silly Bill
45. Silly Bill
46. Unclouded Day
47. Unclouded Day

A Tunes
48. Breakin' Up Christmas
49. Breakin' Up Christmas
50. Cluck Ol' Hen
51. Cluck Ol' Hen
52. Cold Frosty Morning
53. Cold Frosty Morning
54. Dinah
55. Dinah
56. Falls of Richmond
57. Highlander's Farewell
58. Highlander's Farewell
59. Kitchen Girl
60. Kitchen Girl
61. New Castle (Texas)
62. New Castle (Texas)
63. Sail Away, Ladies
64. Sail Away, Ladies
65. Sally Goodin
66. Sally Goodin
67. Sally Goodin (G)
68. Sally Goodin (G)
69. Sheep Shell Corn
70. Sheep Shell Corn
71. Sugar in the Gourd
72. Sugar in the Gourd
73. Train on the Island

Two-Key Tunes
74. Flop-Eared Mule
75. Flop-Eared Mule
76. Jenny Lind Polka
77. Jenny Lind Polka

www.ingramcontent.com/pod-product-compliance
Lightning Source LLC
Chambersburg PA
CBHW042018150426
43197CB00002B/70